A GLITCH IN THE MATRIX

10 Energy Mastery Codes for Becoming the Main Character in Your Life

YASMEEN TURAYHI

Edited by Bailey Potter and Danielle Dorman

For those who want to unhook from the matrix, stop living by other people's scripts, and become the main character of their own story.

For the seekers who sense there is more, even when time, energy, or resources run low, may these pages be a small doorway back to your power.

To those who see through the illusion of the dream-world and choose to stay awake, thank you for remembering your true nature and helping others find their way back.

And to my family, the foundation upon which all things become possible.

Praise for
A GLITCH IN THE MATRIX

"Yasmeen Turayhi's A Glitch in the Matrix is a luminous, high-frequency manual for anyone ready to reclaim authorship of their own story and live as the main character in the great film of consciousness we call life. Yasmeen invites us to laugh at our human patterns, to loosen our grip on control, and to re-enter life as a work of art in motion.

This book is part mystical field guide, part energetic playbook, and part love letter that reconnects you to your original creative power."

—**Arielle Ford**, Author of The Soulmate Secret and Turn Your Mate Into Your Soulmate

"If you're like me, you've spent years in reaction mode, checking boxes, chasing approval, mistaking busyness for purpose. We call this success, but deep down we know something's misfiring in the system. Yasmeen Turayhi exposes that misfire for what it is: a glitch in perception. Drawing on her own wake-up call from her high-velocity Silicon Valley career to a decade of study in energy medicine, Yasmeen outlines a new way to live, from unconscious survival to intentional authorship of reality. Reading it gave me more than codes and tools, it opened my eyes to see."

—**Barnet Bain**, Producer *What DreamsMay Come,*Author of *How to be a Friend (in an Unfriendly World)*

Contents

Preface

When I was a kid, I watched the movie *The Matrix* like most people do—with a low level of awareness. I saw it as just another fascinating science-fiction film, a mix of action and drama with a talented (and undeniably handsome) lead actor.

But something shifted when I rewatched it in my early thirties. It wasn't a conscious decision—I happened to put it on during a flight back to California. This time, however, I experienced it on an entirely different level of awareness. My consciousness had changed, and suddenly, the deeper meaning of the film became glaringly obvious.

I realized *The Matrix* wasn't just a sci-fi movie. It was a metaphor—a documentary on the illusionary system we're all living in. The film laid out, in cinematic form, the nightmare that's occurring on our planet right now. This is why I'll refer to scenes from the movie in each chapter, giving you an example of the teachings each of the ten energy mastery codes provide.

My purpose in writing this book is to provide you with a practical guide—one that helps you understand how energy actually moves and works in your daily life. Because once you start recognizing the simulation for what it is—an illusion—you, too, can begin to reclaim your power.

You see, the simulation affects us all. It was right before I watched *The Matrix* for the second time that I realized, I had lost my spark—the fire that lit me up from the inside. I would often ask myself, *Is this really all there is? Wake up, go to work, and sit in a monotonous cycle?*

Looking back now, I see how asleep I must have been to even ask that question. Because when you truly begin to look — really look — you discover that reality is far richer than what our five senses can perceive. There is so much more happening beneath the surface: more beauty, more mystery, more love. So much more that it moves me to tears just thinking about it. Most people live at the mercy of what they can see and touch, reacting to the world outside them — never realizing that by doing so, they surrender their power to shape the world within.

A little more about me: I'm a filmmaker, an author, a TEDx speaker, three-time podcast host, yogi, and I once ran a tech company in Silicon Valley. I am currently the host of a global podcast called *Gatewaysto Awakening* and run an intuition school called the *Inner Knowing School* (InnerKnowingSchool.com) for executives and creatives, where I teach leaders how to tap into their intuition and master their energy instead of their time. I also have a master certification in intuition medicine, am a yoga teacher, and I've studied energy and natural law for a long time. I'm a student of many teachers who teach different laws of the Universe—the Law of Attraction, the Law of Assumption, the Law of Karma, the Law of Resonance,and many more, and you'll see these teachings reflected throughout my book.

Once I discovered how to reignite my inner spark,I felt a responsibility to sharewhat I've learned with others. And since embracing that calling, I've found an incredible sense of accomplishment and peace in teaching what I've learned over the past fifteen years to my clients and podcast listeners, guiding them to tune their awareness toward the life that they want, rather than sit in default or reactive mode. It's part of what inspired me to write this book. In these pages, you'll find helpful tools to increase your sense of fulfillment and happiness in your life, though the information found in this book is by no means a one-size-fits-all way to heal trauma.

There's a power in deciding your thoughts, in image making. We all have free will and choice in creating our thoughts, and the associated images that go along with them. And no one person or situation can "make you" feel a certain way. You can decide how to feel right now. Life is about being the master of your awareness and learning to hone your feelings.

Today, I choose to live a life of joy, adventure, and purpose.

Would you like to join me?

Introduction

What you know you can't explain, but you feel it. You've felt it your entire life, that there's something wrong with the world. You don't know what it is, but it's there, like a splinter in your mind, driving you mad. It is this feeling that has brought you to me.

—*The Matrix*

Every day, countless people wake up feeling like something essential is missing—not in their material lives but in the way they experience life itself. They're playing out scripts they didn't write, reacting to circumstances they didn't create, and wondering why fulfillment remains just out of reach. But what if the key to a radically different existence lies not in changing your external reality but in transforming how you direct your energy within it? In *A Glitch in the Matrix*, I reveal the hidden codes that govern how reality responds to you—ten codes of energy mastery that, when followed, liberate you from playing a supporting actor role in someone else's production and position you as the main character of your own extraordinary life.

A Glitch in the Matrix

Early on in the movie *The Matrix*, Morpheus offers Neo a choice between two pills: Take the red pill to discover an unsettling truth about reality, or take the blue pill and continue living in a dreamlike state of ignorance. This pivotal scene symbolizes a choice we all face at every moment—whether to remain within the boundaries of our familiar beliefs or awaken to our unlimited power to create.

Once Neo takes the red pill, there's no going back.

He is finally pulled out of the illusion, and instantly, his entire perception of reality shatters. At first, he experiences severe disorientation. His body convulses. His vision distorts. The world around him flickers like a glitching program, and then—he wakes up.

Not in the Matrix. Not in the simulation. But in the real world—a dimly lit, water-filled pod surrounded by endless rows of human batteries, each trapped in a false reality, completely unaware.

Modern Life: A Blue Pill Existence

Most of us have unknowingly opted for the blue pill—a scripted existence where we follow the directions written by others, stay distracted by the background scenery, and never question who's pulling the strings. Inside this limited reality, we fall into one of two predictable scripts: Either we cling to overly familiar roles that feel safe but leave us ultimately uninspired, or we fill our lives with drama, distractions, and chaos because stillness would reveal just how out of alignment we have become. In the first case, our need for predictability is usually born out of fear of change, of uncertainty, of failure, so we engineer our lives for maximum control. But predictability, let's be honest, is boring theater—and choosing a "safe" life is not the same as choosing a life that's in flow and filled with excitement. On the flip side, if we're addicted to busyness, drama and chaos can become our baseline. We mistake intensity for intimacy; adrenaline for aliveness. But chaos is just another form of avoidance. It keeps us moving so fast, we don't have to feel the discomfort underneath.

The Third Option: ConsciousMain Character

What if you didn't have to choose between a boring monologue and a chaotic melodrama? What if there was a way to live with aliveness, spontaneity, and creativity— without burning out or living in constant reactivity? This is the path of living in flow as the conscious main character of your own life.

This role isn't about controlling every detail of the script. It's about cultivating the capacity to improvise and respond to life in real time. It's a state of being where synchronicity becomes the norm, not the exception, where the right people, ideas, and opportunities appear—not because you forced them, but because you became energetically available for them. When you step into main character consciousness, you understand that life is something that flows *from* and *through*you, not something that happens *to* you. You know yourself as the cause, not the effect; as the creator, not the victim. You become the writer, the director, and the producer of your own life's play, the one who summons the intention, who beats the drum that assembles the supporting characters of your unfolding masterpiece.

Success, Self-Sabotage, and a Spiritual Quest

For a long time, I didn't know I was the main character in my own play, and whenever I experienced wild success in one scene, it would invariably be followed by a crash in the next act. In other words, I knew how to create amazing manifestations, but I couldn't sustain that upward movement without some other part of my life falling apart.

Gay Hendricks talks about this phenomenon in his book *The Big Leap*. He suggests that when we go beyond our self-imposed limits of how much good we believe we deserve or can handle in one area of our lives, we unconsciously sabotage our success in other areas.

This pattern was strikingly evident during the years I spent climbing the corporate ladder in Silicon Valley, where I led the successful launch of over two hundred software products and features. On paper, I was living the dream, but something inside wasn't clicking. Every morning, I'd write in my journal about feeling like "an enlightened sheep"—successful by every conventional standard yet deeply disconnected from my purpose.

One day, I did something that shocked everyone around me: I walked away from my cushy executive job with its stock options. My parents actually flew in from

Chicago to see if I'd lost my mind. My friends assured them I was just taking a sabbatical, but deep down, I knew I was answering a call to something greater. That decision launched me into a decade-long quest to understand energy, consciousness, and human potential. I became obsessed with uncovering the hidden codes of life. I deeply wanted to understand why some people seem to live with ease, creativity, and purpose while others struggle in survival and reaction mode.

Along the way, I launched *Gateways to Awakening*, a global podcast where I've had the privilege of conducting in-depth interviews with over 250 renowned thought leaders, pioneering scientists, and esteemed spiritual luminaries, including researchers from institutions such as the Princeton Engineering Anomalies Research Lab and the visionary founders of the HeartMath Institute. From my interviews with these experts and through my own deep dive into their workshops spanning everything from neuroscience to wellness, I began to discern a recurring theme across much of the spiritual and personal development landscape: *Everything we desire in life comes down to managing our energy and living in an internal state of balance.* The energy mastery codes I will teach you throughout this book represent a comprehensive system of knowledge that I have learned and applied over the past fifteen years.

The Quantum Field of All Possibilities

Before I introduce the ten codes for becoming the main character of your life, let me share the foundational understanding that serves as the bedrock for all conscious creation.

There exists a field of infinite potential that mystics, scientists, and philosophers throughout human existence have sought to name and understand. Freud called it "the unconscious." Jung referred to it as "the collective unconscious." Quantum physicists describe it as the "non-local field;" Eastern traditions revere it as "prana," "Chi," or "the Tao." Some spiritual seekers recognize it as "the Akashic records." Mystics may experience it as "Spirit," "Mother Nature," or "Unity Consciousness," and researchers at the frontier of science measure it as the "zero-point field." All of these are simply different names used in an attempt to describe the same profound reality that underlies all existence. And this quantum field isn't just a philosophical concept—it's a living reality of infinite potential waiting for your awareness to shape it.

Drawing from the many-worlds interpretation theory in quantum physics, we can understand that infinite possibilities exist simultaneously. Every choice you make navigates you through this field of potential, activating certain timelines while deactivating others. Your inner frequency tunes, like a radio station, to a possibility in the field. Imagine your life as an ancient towering tree with countless far-reaching branches. Every choice you make determines which "branch" your consciousness follows: When you choose your career path, the branch where you became a doctor still exists, even though you're now experiencing life as a teacher. When you decide to move to New York instead of staying in your hometown, both versions of your life continue to unfold in parallel realities, even though you're only conscious of one.

Within this infinite field exist countless versions of you—the prosperous you, the struggling you, the partnered you, the lonely you, the vibrant you, the depleted you. The version you're experiencing right now, in this moment, is just one expression of your limitless potential.

What this means is different versions of you exist at different frequency states. When you vibrate at the frequency of compassion, you naturally encounter different circumstances, people, and opportunities than when you operate from anger, guilt, or shame. Your inner state—your thoughts, beliefs, and especially your feelings—functions as the predictive engine that determines which experiences manifest in your reality. This reveals a profound truth: Rather than trying to manipulate your external world, the most efficient path to transformation is shifting your inner frequency. *When you change your energetic state, your reality must reorganize itself to match.*

It's essential to understand that this is *not* an intellectual exercise; it's a practice requiring consistent application. And these practices are the basis of the methodology I've developed—combining neuroscience, meditation, and energy-shifting techniques—which have transformed my life and those of my clients. Because while it's true that we all begin life at different frequency baselines influenced by our upbringing and even patterns of intergenerational trauma, I've witnessed remarkable shifts in people from all backgrounds and starting points.

As my colleague Renée Garcia insightfully observes, "Everyone has a theory on reality, and there's evidence to support all theories." This is because reality doesn't discriminate—it simply reflects your frequency back to you. In other words, you don't attract what you want; you attract what you energetically broadcast. So, why continue operating on limited or destructive programs when you could upgrade your inner software to align with your highest potential?

The Blueprint for Your Starring Role

As a preview of the journey ahead, the following pages detail each of the ten "codes" that will transform you from a supporting role to the leading protagonist in your own life's story. Each principle builds upon the last, creating a comprehensive framework for reclaiming your creative power and authoring your own story. After experimenting with these ten energy mastery codes in my own life and witnessing their impact, I decided to write this book as a love letter to anyone who wants to master their time and energy and understand natural law and the codes of our reality. These aren't just theoretical concepts—they're practical tools I've tested and refined through years of personal practice and work with clients. As you explore each rule presented in each chapter, you'll discover not only the "why" behind these energy codes but also the "how"—specific practices to integrate them into your daily life. Consider this your roadmap to conscious creation, with each principle revealing another dimension of your untapped potential.

Here, then, are the ten codes to becoming the main character of your life:

Code #1: With Full Acceptance, You Unlock Your Power to Create

When you fully accept your life exactly as it is, without resistance or judgment, you step into your creative power. Most people waste precious energy fighting what has already happened, staying trapped in loops of blame, regret, and bitterness. Acceptance isn't resignation—it's the first key to true liberation. By embracing reality as it is rather than as you wish it to be, you reclaim the energy you've been leaking into the past and redirect it toward creating what you truly desire. Like Neo in *The Matrix*, your transformation begins not when you wish for change but when you loosen your attachment to fixed outcomes and open your vision to new possibilities you couldn't see before.

Code #2: Embodiment Is the Portal to Mastery

True power lies in being fully present and grounded in your physical body. When you're embodied, all your scattered energy returns to you, allowing you to access your full potential. Most people live disconnected—their bodies are present while their awareness drifts elsewhere, leaving them depleted and unable to direct their energy with intention. Through grounding practices that connect you to the Earth's frequency, you stabilize your energy and become the most powerful person in any room—not because you're the loudest or the richest but because you're fully *here*. This embodied presence creates safety for others, enhances your intuition, and becomes the foundation for all other energy work.

Code #3: Levity and Letting Go to Create Space to Receive

The moment you stop gripping life so tightly, everything you desire flows toward you with ease. Most people create energetic distortion by making things too important, leading to tension, resistance, and blockages in their natural flow. When you lower the importance you place on outcomes and approach life with lightness and humor, you remove the very resistance that was keeping your desires at bay. In the same way that a clenched fist can't hold anything new, your energy cannot receive if you're contracted around what you want. True manifestation isn't about forcing, controlling, or trying harder—it's about creating space through letting go and leading with levity.

Code #4: What You Identify with, You Become

Your self-concept determines your entire experience of reality—meaning, you cannot manifest anything beyond what you believe about yourself. The unconscious identity you've constructed from past experiences, cultural conditioning, and others' opinions acts like an invisible ceiling on what's possible in your life. By intentionally choosing a self-concept that's aligned with your desires, you step into a new reality where that expanded version of you already exists. This isn't merely positive thinking—it's a fundamental shift in who you believe yourself to be. When you change your inner conversations and embody a new identity with certainty, the external world has no choice but to reflect this transformation back to you.

Code #5: You Have Agency over Your Feelings, so Choose Certainty

Your feeling states are the true creative force shaping your reality, and they're entirely within your control. While temporary emotions may arise in response to external events, your sustained feeling states are conscious choices that determine what you magnetize into your life. The world rewards certainty above all else—when you cultivate absolute faith in your desired outcome, reality rearranges itself to match your conviction. By deciding how you'll feel at the end of each day and directing your awareness toward that feeling regardless of circumstances, you create a resonance that attracts matching experiences. Your emotional frequency becomes your signature broadcast to the Universe, bringing back to you precisely what you transmit.

Code #6: Your Outer Reality Is a Mirror of Your Inner World

Everything you experience externally is a reflection of your internal state—your beliefs, thoughts, and emotional vibration. Most people try to change the mirror of external circumstances without changing what's being reflected—their inner world. This Mirror Principle operates like karma but often comes with a time delay: The energy you send out returns, often when you least expect it. When you stand in judgement, make yourself more or less important than other people, or create energetic hierarchies, the Universe will restore balance, sometimes painfully. Instead of reacting to what appears in your mirror, recognize it as feedback about your inner state and redirect your focus to what you want to create instead.

Code #7: Listen to Your Heart for Signs of Alignment

Your heart is the true CEO of your life, not your mind. And when your heart and mind achieve coherence, you access a deeper intelligence that guides you toward your authentic path. Physical sensations of expansion, lightness, and freedom indicate alignment with your soul's purpose, while contraction, heaviness, and resistance signal misalignment. Most people make decisions based solely on logic or social conditioning, ignoring these vital energetic signals from their heart. By tuning in to what feels energetically expansive rather than what seems rational, you tap into a level of wisdom beyond mental processing, allowing synchronicity to become your norm and attracting opportunities aligned with your highest good.

Code #8: Recast Your Inner Critic as Your Inner Coach

We all have an inner narrator—that internal voice that provides a running commentary on our lives all day long. What you may not realize is that this voice shapes your reality more powerfully than almost any external force. If you allow this voice to become your harshest critic, you'll unconsciously sabotage your desires with doubt, fear, and limitation. But by consciously transforming this inner narrator into a supportive coach and best friend, you create an internal environment of encouragement and certainty. This shift isn't about superficial positive thinking but about recognizing that your relationship with yourself is the foundation of every other relationship and experience. When you consistently choose empowering inner conversations that align with your desired reality, your external world naturally shifts to match this new narrative.

Code #9: Intention, Prayer, and Future-Self Scripting

You have the ability to direct universal energy through focused intention, heartfelt prayer, and embodied future-self practices. By setting clear intentions, you command energy to move in specific directions. Through prayer, you amplify this directive with emotional power. And by writing from your future self's perspective—as if your desires have already manifested—you program your subconscious mind to notice and act upon opportunities that are aligned with this vision. Unlike wishful thinking, these practices involve feeling the reality of your desires so completely that your nervous system begins responding as if they're already true. This energetic time travel allows you to step into the version of yourself that has already achieved what you're creating.

Code #10: To Remain in Harmony with the Universe, You Must Expand Along with It

The Universe is in a constant state of expansion, and to live in alignment with it, you must continuously expand your consciousness as well. When you contract through fear, materialism, or self-focus, you move against the natural flow of creation. Creativity is not a luxury but a necessity. It is an act of intuitive communion with a field larger than the self. Drawing from yogic wisdom and Anodea Judith's teachings on the sacral chakra, creative flow arises when we honor the body's natural rhythms of pleasure, desire, and curiosity.

True legacy comes from shifting from individual success to collective elevation. As you master these energy principles, your focus will naturally expand beyond personal gain to how your creative gifts serve the whole. By measuring success not by what you accumulate but by what you contribute, you align with the Universe's expansive nature and discover that your highest fulfillment comes from being a conduit for something greater than yourself.

Throughout this book, I will invite you to approach these energy mastery practices with a spirit of playful experimentation. If you're skeptical, that's fine; I'm not asking for blind belief. You'll find actionable rituals throughout the chapters, which will walk you through the process of embracing each of the ten codes. Simply try these codes as an experiment in your own life and observe what happens. This is an invitation, not a prescription; a framework for you to adapt to your unique experience rather than another set of rigid commandments to follow. My deepest hope is that you have fun with this process.

By the time you reach the end of this book, you will experience what Neo felt in the final scene of *The Matrix*—that moment of profound awakening when you realize you are not just a passive character in someone else's story but the conscious creator of your own reality, of your own life's movie. These ten energy mastery codes will transform how you navigate every aspect of life—from relationships to purpose, from setbacks to success. You'll stop forcing, struggling, and reacting to whatever appears in your path and instead flow with a newfound certainty that comes from true energetic alignment.

The world won't suddenly change overnight, but *you* will. And that changes everything. The obstacles that once seemed insurmountable will reveal themselves as opportunities for expansion. The limitations you accepted as truth will dissolve in the face of your evolving self-concept. You will discover that you are the one you've been waiting for all along—the director of your life's performance, the author of your own story, the master of your energy. This isn't just another self-help promise; it's an invitation to reclaim your innate power and expand along with the expansion of the Universe itself.

So, if you're ready to take the red pill—to reveal the hidden codes of reality our modern world has forgotten to teach you—let's embark on this journey together.

CHAPTER 1

Code #1: In Full Acceptance, You Unlock Your Power to Create

Your reactions, whether positive or negative, are creative of future circumstances.
—Neville Goddard

Once you fully accept your life thus far, then the rest of your life can truly begin.

In the movie *The Matrix*, Neo initially refuses to believe he is The One. He is stuck in victimhood, doubting his abilities and feeling powerless against the system. The moment he accepts reality—dodging bullets and seeing beyond his perceived limitations—he shifts from victimhood to empowerment.

This is the essence of acceptance: It is the first step toward freedom.

Many people waste years, even decades, resisting their reality—fighting what already happened rather than using that energy to shape what comes next.

Neo didn't become The One by wishing—he became The One by accepting. Once he stopped fighting what was and stepped into what *is*, he could bend reality to his will.

In this chapter, we examine the first of the ten energy mastery codes, which explores how to step out of victimhood and outrage and instead choose radical acceptance. Only then can you take what *is*, own it, and unlock the power to rewrite your life.

Acceptance vs. Victimhood

To navigate the infinite possibilities available to us, we must first acknowledge and accept everything that has happened up until this point.

It will be nearly impossible to truly embrace and act upon the other nine rules unless you're willing to accept your past. Acceptance is the first key to true liberation and empowerment.

But let's be clear: Acceptance is not resignation. It is not passive. It does not mean agreement. It is an active acknowledgment of the present moment—an embrace of reality as it *is*, not as we wish it to be.

It is an embracing of reality without resistance or judgment. When we resist reality, we become trapped— stuck in loops of suffering, pouring energy into something that has already happened.

The Cost of Resistance

I once worked with a client who was going through a divorce, and she could not accept the end of her relationship. She was stuck in the past, replaying both good and bad memories of the relationship with an emphasis on the last year of arguments that culminated in a big blowout. She was filled with regret and nostalgia about the last twenty years she spent with her ex and how it had never dawned on her that he would leave her.

We've all met people like this. Something happened to them one, twenty or even fifty years ago, and their reaction to the event seems like it was just yesterday. Their emotional state is fresh, as if the drama was still happening.

I knew that any attempt at communicating the codes of life with her would fall on deaf ears in her current state. She had simply not accepted her current reality. Her current reality did not reflect that her ex was no longer her partner and that he had moved on. She was stuck in a frame.

She was leaking energy into a reality that no longer existed, though it was one she no longer even really wanted.

Until she could accept this new reality, she would continue to waste a tremendous amount of her precious energy and feel drained. That energy could have been re-invested back into herself and her own life, but instead, she chose to spend it on him.

At any given moment, we are either:

- **Spending our energy**—wasting it on things beyond our control, ruminating, complaining, and regretting; or
- **Investing our energy**—redirecting it into building what we do want.

The majority of people on the planet are constantly spending their energy. Their thoughts, attention, and awareness go to an energy source that is ultimately unprofitable and nonreciprocal rather than to whatever life they're trying to build and develop. They blame the outside world for how they feel, believing that "They made me feel this way," "If only things had gone differently, I'd be happy," and "This ruined my life." I've seen so many people waste a tremendous amount of time playing defense in life, complaining about what's happening, rather than leading their life and directing the flow of energy toward what they want instead.

But the truth is, no one can *make* you feel anything. Even that language assumes that another person's words or actions control you somehow, like a puppet master.

But your emotions and your feelings are *your* responsibility.

We must learn to take full control over our own emotional inner world, our reactions, and our programs—and not place blame on the outside world. For every time we react emotionally, we give away our energy. Of course, people and situations can challenge us and cross our boundaries, but it's our place to state when someone has crossed our personal boundaries and make a choice on how we want to respond.

When something triggers you, it pulls you into its energy field—and that's how you remain stuck in repetitive cycles. If you don't want an experience or behavior to repeat in your life, you'll need to stop reacting to it in kind. The more you *react,* the more you reinforce that reality.

But you are not a victim of life. There is a different way. You can choose to *create* a new reality.

Breaking Free from the Matrix

Every life has its own "script," and many are performing their life from a script someone else—like their parents, teachers, religious groups, community, and social media—wrote for them. Very few people on the planet have written their own script for the life that they truly want.

A decade ago, I had been deeply entrenched in a technology career in Silicon Valley. During my journey, I had a number of creative aspirations, yet the demands of my full-time career consumed all of my time and energy. By the end of the day, I was left with only fumes and would feel drained.

One day, while doing Julia Cameron's Morning Pages exercise where one writes a three-page-long stream of consciousness, I came to a realization: I had been writing the same reflections every single day for over six months.

Specifically, I wrote about how I was an enlightened sheep.

Here is the entry:

Diary Entry: 2016, San Francisco

Some days, I feel like I'm swimming against the current. Each stroke takes more and more effort. I know that I am capable of great things in life, and I want so much more than what I feel I must do, which is work at a company and for a job that I'm not entirely excited about or interested in. I need to just be honest with myself. Why am I so scared of the unknown?

Maybe because the unknown is terrifying and scary, and it's totally outside of my control. Or maybe I feel like I might chase something more important and idealize it, and find it's just as empty as what I ran away from and find myself right back where I started. Or maybe I just need to stop chasing anything at all.

There's a drum inside me that beats for something truer. When I follow it, I feel alive, electric, present, free. But most days, I quiet it down, letting what is comfortable and safe drown it out. I trade curiosity for comfort, and truth for stability.

I wish I could ignore the pull and graze like the other sheep, but I can't. I know what it feels like to betray myself. And every time I do, I drift a little further from who I really am. Maybe the work now is to stop choosing what's safe, and start following the sound of that drum, wherever it leads.

I always feel emotional when I re-read that entry, because that was a huge turning point on my path. And months later, I decided to choose something different and left the corporate world.

At the time, I could no longer look at my Morning Pages entries without feeling a sense of misalignment deep within my soul. I couldn't keep writing the same scene of my life. I needed to take a step into the unknown. So one day, I walked out of my executive job in a successful tech company, both literally and figuratively.

For about a month, I felt liberated on a level that I had not experienced my entire adult life. Yet after a month passed, I started to unwind and privately wondered what I would do about income after a while, especially since I lived in such an expensive city and neighborhood in San Francisco.

I decided to fly to Bali for an impromptu *Eat Pray Love* adventure and signed up for surf camp. Right before I left, I realized that my nerves were starting to bother me; I was feeling the emotional weight of my decision and wondered if I made the right choice or if I was being irresponsible.

The big change happened when I did, well, nothing. I stopped thinking and worrying, and I let go. I let *go* completely.

In a moment of surrender, I asked myself what would happen if I accepted my life as it was and surrendered to the present moment. In that instant, a sense of lightness washed over me, and I realized that worrying about the future served me no purpose.

Once I could embrace the unknown, I let go of the chatter in my mind and found peace in the present. Though my external circumstances remained unchanged, internally, I felt a profound shift toward greater clarity and acceptance.

And once I let go, my external world began to bloom. My phone started to ring and two new clients emerged seemingly out of nowhere, who paid me as much as I made full time for working part-time. I also got the flexibility I needed at that time to work remotely and dive deep into the world of personal development.

This technique is one that I go back to often. When I begin to feel that anxiety again or when fear starts to accumulate, I let go and surrender to the here and now. Energy cannot move if we are holding onto it tightly and contracting our energy. It's as if the energy in the world can't find us if we contract.

Two years later, it happened again.

I had always wanted to create a spirituality podcast. I attempted to record an episode by myself, but the quality was terrible. The audio was off balance, my pacing was awkward, and I cringed just listening to it. I knew it wasn't good enough, so I let it go. I let go, detached from the outcome, and diverted my attention to other things. I knew I still wanted to create the show, but I let go of how it would manifest. We'll discuss the value of letting go of expectations more in chapter 3.

A year later, I met a podcast network. I wasn't looking for them. I wasn't pitching my idea. They found me, and they had a proposal. They wanted me to create a podcast—on spirituality and consciousness. It was the exact show I had envisioned. The only difference was that this time, I wouldn't have to do it alone. The network would handle the production. They would take care of the sound engineering, the editing, and the logistics. All I had to do was show up, host the show, and find the guests.

I hadn't forced it. I hadn't chased it. I had simply let it go.

And then there was the film.

For years, I had been sitting on a short film script. It was something I had written with the intention of bringing to life, yet I had no idea how to make it happen. The film industry felt like an impenetrable world, and I had no connections, no roadmap, and no clear way forward.

So I let it go.

One evening, I attended a birthday party in San Francisco. I wasn't thinking about my film. I wasn't networking. I wasn't trying to get it made. I was simply present, enjoying the night.

Then, I met someone.

We started talking, and somehow, the conversation led to my script. He asked to read it, and I sent it to him the next day. He fell in love with it immediately. Without hesitation, he committed to helping me bring it to life. That night, I had unknowingly met my future business partner.

Together, we would go on to create an award-winning short film.

None of it happened through force. None of it required struggle or strain. The more I relaxed, the more life responded.

This is the lesson: Energy cannot move if we are contracting around it.

Most people hold on too tightly to the things they want. They push, they force, they obsess. They try to control every variable, every outcome, every step along the way. But energy does not flow toward tension. When we hold on too tightly, we block the very thing we are trying to create.

Letting go is not about giving up. It is about creating space.

It is trusting that when we release the need to control every detail, life has a way of arranging things far better than we ever could.

It is the opposite of passivity—it is the deepest kind of alignment.

The moment you stop clenching, the moment you stop gripping, life finally has room to reach back. Because energy flows where it is given space to move.

In many cases, the universal flow of energy has a much better plan than any mind could come up with. This was the point where my life began to improve in ways I never expected it to.

I had initially believed that I had to work in a corporate job and rise up the ranks because that was the assembly-line script that most of our western culture adheres to. But deep down, I understood that this kind of life was rigged against me and would produce a rather uneventful life.

Had I continued, I would not have gotten to know myself or my inner world. I would likely have gotten to the end of my life and wondered, "So what was that all for?" But I knew I wanted flexibility, freedom, and creative agency. I had simply been running on an outdated program and software, and I had finally found the courage to live a way of life that served *me:* I had let go and decided to accept my life, exactly as it is.

Most people are afraid of leaving the familiar because they don't know what's on the other side of their decision. Novelty, the new and the unknown, has its risks. But does your mediocre past really outweigh the limitless potential of your future?

Leave the Past in the Past

For today, look at the past and decide that you will leave it where it belongs, and accept your life as it is.

Rupert Spira, a renowned teacher in the field of non-duality, often explores the nature of time and our relationship to the past. In one conversation, he asked someone, "Have you ever been to the past?" The answer, of course, is no. The past does not exist. What exists is your mind's recreation of it, in this moment. Imagine a moving train, but that train is *you.* You cannot stop the train and go backward. You cannot return to the past. You can only pull your energy back from it.

In other words, the past is not something we can directly access or visit. It exists only as a thought or memory arising in the present moment. We don't experience the past itself—we experience a current mental or emotional image of what we call "the past." The past is nothing more than a concept occurring here and now.

In order to harness your full energy, you must pull your energy out of the past. With acceptance, you can cultivate a sense of resilience and claim back your energy from the past, bringing it into the only place that matters: the present moment. And the more energy you reclaim from the past, the more power you have in the present moment and ultimately, your future.

Some of us feel shame or guilt based on what we may have done in the past. Some of us even feel shame for how *others* have treated us in the past. In many cases, others may have hurt us deeply without any good reason. But by sitting in resentment and anger, we actually hurt ourselves rather than the other person; we give our energy to the other person rather than invest it in ourselves. It reminds me of a well-known saying: "Resentment is like drinking poison and then hoping it will kill your enemies." There's no benefit in resentment.

On my podcast episode about biogeometry, Doreya Karim gives us a handy map for understanding the different ways we can experience time. She invites us to stop thinking of "time" as a single thing and choose the lens we use: 1) the clocked world of *linear time*, 2) the seasonal ebb and flow of *cyclical time*, or 3) the deeper, non-chronological field she calls *stacked time*—the place where emotional- and meaning-based charges live and replay, beyond dates and facts. These are not just memories, but unresolved energetic echoes, the lingering charge left by an experience that was too overwhelming, or too incomplete to fully process in the moment. They live outside of linear time, waiting to be felt, witnessed, and transformed.

Where Spira shows that the past is a present-moment thought, Doreya explains *how* that thought can continue to tug on your life: It becomes a resonance pattern that keeps returning until you change its quality. This matters because leaving the past in the past is not the same as pretending it didn't happen. It's an energetic choice.

When we refuse to endlessly rerun old hurts, we reclaim the attention, fuel, and creative energy that were being siphoned away. Doreya's work points to a practical reflection: You cannot always change what happened, but you can change the emotional-mental pattern that carries the event forward. In other words, you can change the *resonance* of the past.

So, how do you do that without getting stuck in "should" or self-blame? You use the right "time" lens. If the thing is a project or deadline, work in linear time. If it's a pattern that cycles every season, honor the cyclical rhythms and give your nervous system permission to rest. If it's a stubborn charge that keeps replaying—grief, shame, a wound that colors relationships—treat it as stacked time: Meet it at the level of its meaning, not with facts but with practices that shift emotional resonance.

Integrating Our Shadow

And as for feeling shame because we may have hurt others, we have to acknowledge that we all have both shadow and light within us. We've likely hurt others and have been hurt by others for the exact same reason, for it's easier to point out what's wrong in others than to see what's wrong in ourselves. I knew someone once who told me that he could not "accept another person's shadow." However, if you cannot accept other people's shadows, you likely cannot accept your own either.

Shadow work is some of the most important work one must do in this lifetime. Every person has both positive and negative qualities, but one's shadow is not necessarily made up of purely "bad" qualities—the shadow often represents one's repressed qualities too. As one of my previous podcast guests Dr. Connie Zweigh, who was a Jungian therapist who coauthored the book *Romancing the Shadow*, said, "The gold is in the shadow." While many of us are naturally afraid of our shadows, whether because someone told us to be afraid or ashamed of them or not, they are simply another side of who we are, and if we push down those parts of ourselves, then we are only inhibiting ourselves from reaching our truest potential.

In order to harness your full energetic signature, you must pull your energy out of the past and accept both the shadow and light within you. Along with this acceptance of the full parts of ourselves, we can also make space for others to be who they are, without needing to control, fix, or judge them. I believe that if you cannot accept your own shadow side, it is nearly impossible to accept another persons shadow side. Everyone is on their own path, and you are only responsible for your own thoughts, feelings, and energy. When uncomfortable feelings come up, remind yourself that they are simply just data points; they are not signaling the need for a reaction. When judgment or intensity surfaces, bring your attention into the body and gently ask: *What is this part trying to show or tell me?* In that inquiry, you can transform these feelings and your energy becomes integrated and whole again.

I believe feelings are something we must learn to hone and integrate, which I'll discuss in chapter 5, but if you feel provoked by someone or something, the easiest thing to do is to pull your attention away from them. Your reactions pull you *into* a field of energy rather than away from it. If you do not want an experience or behavior to repeat itself in your life, I would suggest not showing a lot of emotion or reacting to it. Indifference is actually a sign of growth. When you stop reacting to things that once triggered you, such as old fears or insecurities, I believe it means you've transcended into a new state of enlightenment.

Building Resilience Instead of Boundaries

These days, it seems like almost everyone is offended by some person, place, or situation at any given time. Without some conflict taking up real estate in our lives, many of us don't know what to do with ourselves.

I understand that this is an oversimplification for some people. For those who have traumatic experiences from the past, I encourage you to stay with me until the end of this book. It's important, of course, to process our feelings and emotional states and hold them sacred. The story— how we interpret our reality—we tell ourselves and attach to these emotional states is not, however, important.

When we do not state our boundaries, our relationship with the world slowly starts to crumble. Every time we do not explicitly share our preferences, we compromise and go into resentment. Over time, resentment becomes a form of victimhood. We place blame on the outer world (a person, a situation) rather than take responsibility for how we showed up. No one wins when there is resentment.

And with resentment, we blame others and create hard boundaries. We've become a culture that is obsessed with creating boundaries instead of improving their resilience. It's important to have healthy boundaries, especially when dealing with toxic people and situations, but I've observed that a number of people lean on their boundaries so much that they lack the social skills and tools to deal with difficult situations and conversations anymore.

Build an inner resilience and indifference to other people's bad behaviors, and you'll have more power and agency over yourself. This is part of accepting what *is* without reacting—keeping your energy focused on *you* rather than giving it to others to spend. Building an inner resilience will also help you with pulling back your reactions.

We All Give Different Meaning to the Exact Same Scene

I have found that most people often experience a very different version of reality from each other in the same exact scenarios. I understand that we all have different lives and worries, but what many don't realize is how they can choose to control their reactions to situations. I don't mean that they can control what's happening externally around them but *internally*. If only they could accept what is occurring and move on instead of getting upset. This makes all the difference for their flow of energy in the day moving forward.

I find so many examples of this where I used to live in Los Angeles, especially at my favorite coffee shop on Montana Street. I often observe people while I sit and drink my coffee and wonder what types of thoughts or inner conversations people are having with themselves: *Are they happy? Are they ruminating on the past? Are they excited about a project they're working on in the present?* Some people are obviously irritated by the long wait at the coffee shop, and others seem more relaxed and composed, and even joyful.

I also love observing how people react to the baristas when the line is long. Some barely acknowledge them, while others lash out in frustration. I made it a habit to greet baristas by name, ask about their day, and radiate good energy. Over time, I noticed a shift—free drinks appeared unexpectedly and gestures of kindness found their way to me, all without any particular reason.

You see, we all chose to stop and get a coffee, but rather than playing the victim—*Why is this line so long? Why can't the barista hurry up?*—I see the wait as a gift. Instead of losing energy to frustration, I use the time for a mini meditation practice. I know that irritation or annoyance would only drain me, and I refuse to waste my energy on something so trivial.

Acceptance.

Accepting life as it is, not as we think it should be.

I have learned to guard my energy carefully. Instead of *spending* energy on unnecessary reactions, I focus on *investing* it in people, places, and experiences that truly matter. And that invested energy seems to always find its way back to me one way or another.

So how about you? Who or what are you spending your energy on in this moment? Do you have full control over your awareness and thoughts? Do you have agency over your inner dialogue and inner conversations? Or are you still in resistance?

Resistance Keeps Energy Stuck

Because many of us do not truly accept ourselves or our lives, we are in resistance to our current situation. The resistance often gets stronger with age. We resist our childhoods or our family, or we regret the choices we've made in the past or wonder what may have happened if we made a different choice about a situation.

Resistance is a psychological defense mechanism where a person unconsciously (or consciously) avoids change or emotional processing. It often manifests as:

- Denial or avoidance (e.g., skipping therapy, changing the subject)
- Intellectualization (overanalyzing feelings instead of feeling them)
- Emotional numbness (dissociation or shutting down)
- Physical symptoms (tension, fatigue, nausea)
- Defensive reactions (rejections, refusals)

I once had a friend who would fall asleep (literally) every time I would talk about topics on acceptance and elevating his consciousness. It was clear his ego (mind) was protecting him from exploring new ideas and possibilities, keeping him numb and static. I say this without judgment; it's not my place nor anyone's place to judge whether someone is ready to explore a wider perspective. All we can do is be an example to others, and perhaps that might inspire them to start asking questions.

This resistance costs us in the accounting ledger of energy in our lives. An old story or script can end up controlling much of our daily experience and, in the long term, our lives. These scripts often act like prison sentences rather than events that happened to us a long time ago.

Acceptance is not spiritual bypassing—which occurs when one uses spiritual concepts to avoid engaging with uncomfortable emotions, personal responsibility, or necessary healing work—nor does it mean agreement. You can accept your life and not agree with the decisions you've made in the past or how events unfolded. True acceptance is a profound act of self-love, self-respect, and forgiveness, allowing us to release the grip of past traumas and reclaim our energy from old wounds.

Many people hang onto the past not only through victimization but also by catastrophizing and dramatizing any and every small and minor inconvenience, and reliving events that happened to them a long time ago. Of course, there is real suffering in the world and everyone deserves the chance to heal from trauma, and I fully acknowledge that, but to constantly rehash a minor inconvenience as if it were a life-altering traumatizing experience is not a great use of our time and certainly not a wise investment of energy.

The energy of acceptance is deeply calming, and from an energetic perspective, it pulls your disassociated and scattered energy back to you from different people, situations, and past frames. Collecting your energy back is a crucial step to master before learning about all the other energy codes of life. When you live fully in the present moment, you operate as a whole, fully integrated human being—one who can access their full power and begin to create the life they want.

Continuing to reinforce past grievances and hurts just reinforces older emotions that are not serving your highest good. An exercise that works well is to sit in a feeling without labeling it or giving it a story. So for example, if you feel the emotion of fear bubbling up, instead of trying to understand it, allow it to be there and let go of your resistance to the feeling. Sit with it for as long as is needed. If you have stored-up emotions, then this may need to become a daily practice until those feelings no longer feel like anchors in your physical body.

You are not the victim of your circumstances. Yet in today's world, playing the victim in life has become a widely popular way to justify staying stuck. It's comforting to justify and explain every single thing that happened to us because it's in the external and outside of us. We've been taught to believe that our outside world reigns supreme and that we are mere victims of our circumstances.

In reality, we have forgotten our true divinity and our power. By playing victim, we give our power away to the past instead of surrendering to life.

Surrendering to Life

Most of us are never really ready to surrender to life. And yet when we do, everything gets easier. What would happen right now, if you decided to just let go?

It's my dream for every single person on Earth to realize the extent of the power they have at their disposal. My desire is that you will become your own therapist, best friend, oracle, cheerleader, and champion. And by being one's own dear friend, we can be better prepared to show up and be a light for others and our communities.

When we give our power away entirely to the outside world and the past, we become slaves to it. Our attention is not our own, and in a way, we *do* become victims. But that is our choice.

So how do we escape the prison of victimhood? It requires a shift in identity, thoughts, and frequency, which I'll discuss more deeply in later chapters. Once you shift your mindset from victimhood to acceptance, you are on your way to becoming the creator of your life.

As for my client who was stuck in her divorce loop, she wasted another year of her life ruminating about the past and could not fully be open to the present moment and what could emerge.

I've seen this occur a lot. It's much easier to place blame on a past event and sabotage our own futures because we would rather stay stuck in a miserable story loop than let go and allow the unknown to create a new story for us. Some of us are even addicted to our own unhappiness and have spent so much of our lives in a negative emotional state that we simply don't feel comfortable when the tides of fate turn toward greener pastures. What's even worse is how when we run negative thought loops, we attract more negativity in our lives. We will explore this more in chapter 6. But for now, I ask that you trust me and let go of the past.

Ritual:

How to Reclaim Your Power

This section is meant to provide you with actionable steps to reclaim your power and embrace the first energy mastery code. Safety note: If you have a history of complex trauma, know that these steps are helpful but not a replacement for trauma-informed therapy. Move at your pace and use grounding tools if anything feels overwhelming.

1. Stop telling the story by default.

Action now: When you catch yourself rehearsing the grievance, say silently: "Pause—that's the story." Then, take one slow breath and notice what's happening in your body.

2. Name the feeling—not the culprit.

Action now: For example, swap "They made me angry" with "I feel anger in my chest." This shifts you from blaming to sensing.

3. Take 100 percent boundary responsibility.

Action now: Pick one small boundary you can set in the next twenty-four hours (mute a thread, leave a conversation, say "no thanks").

4. Make a micro-action list (not a rant list).

Action now: Write three tiny, practical steps you can take to change your situation—one physical, one social, one administrative.

5. Refuse rumination on command.

Action now: Set a five-minute "rumination window" later today—when the loop starts, gently say, "Not now," and do a sixty-second breathing reset.

6. Neutralize the charge.

Action now: Say five objective truths about yourself and five objective truths about the other person or situation to disconnect from the field.

7. Ask for what you need—directly.

Action now: Pick one person and request one clear, small support from them (For example: "Can you hold me accountable and call me tomorrow?" or "Can you be my texting buddy for the next few weeks?"). The practice of asking breaks helplessness.

Once you fully accept your life, the next step is to embody that acceptance—to integrate what you know, to ground yourself in the present, and to fully inhabit your own body. So with that, let's move on to the next of the ten energy mastery codes of life: grounding and embodiment.

CHAPTER 2

Code #2: Embodiment and Grounding is the Portal to Mastery

Grounding is the cornerstone of energetic health—it stabilizes your spirit in your body and connects you to the infinite wisdom of the Earth.

—Dr. Francesca McCartney

Neo steps into the training simulation. He doesn't quite get it yet—his mind is still tethered to the old world. Morpheus beats him easily and watches him struggle, then drops the question that shatters his perception: "Do you think that's air you're breathing now?"

Neo pauses. His energy is scattered, ungrounded. He knows the matrix isn't real—intellectually. But knowing something and embodying it in the body are two different things.

Then it clicks. He stops overthinking. He drops into his body and his breathing slows. And suddenly, his movements are effortless. He no longer fights against the illusion—he moves *through* it. His power isn't just in his mind. It's in every fiber of his being. His eyes literally and figuratively open.

This chapter examines how embodying what you know, not just conceptually understanding it, can lead you to a level of mastery you didn't previously have. You don't just know something—you *become* it. We also explore what grounding means and ways to practice it. For when you are fully *grounded* in your awareness—when your mind, body, and energy become one—you can unlock your full potential.

Power Comes from Within

The most powerful person in the room is not the most successful, richest, or even the loudest. Instead, it is the most present and grounded person. An embodied and grounded person has all of their energy and power at their disposal and can direct it in any way they want. This person often has a calm, quiet presence, and everyone feels safe and secure in their presence. We intuitively trust people who are grounded and embodied.

This is partly due to our ability to transfer energy, even though we may not be aware of it all the time. Our energy, whether it's positive or negative, constantly affects the nervous systems of those around us, so we immediately feel more grounded in the presence of a grounded person. It physically feels good to interact with someone who has a regulated and calm nervous system, and we feel safe when we feel congruency between the way their body moves and the words that come out of their mouth. When a yes means a full-body *yes*; when a no means a full-body *no*.

I believe we are all striving to live a life that is in alignment, integration, and wholeness. This is the state of embodiment that feels good in our physical body. And when we feel safe and secure in whatever we're doing and wherever we are and grounded, we're connected to the present moment. This is when we have the most power.

Without grounding, our energy is dispersed. We may be physically present, but our awareness is elsewhere. And when we're not truly here, we give our power away.

The Illusion of Success

When I was in my early thirties, I worked for a technology startup in Silicon Valley. I had moved from NYC to San Francisco a few years earlier and immersed myself in the world of technology and commercializing products. I felt like a cast member in the HBO documentary, *Silicon Valley*. At the time, I was obsessed with the physical and material world, or as mystics like Neville Goddard call it, "the world of Caesar." I felt like I needed validation and material success in order to be happy and fulfilled.

My soul, however, was asleep.

I was not driven or motivated by inspiration but fear.

After the spontaneous spiritual awakening I described in the last chapter, followed by a decade long inquiry of personal development, I learned that all the material and outward success in the world would never give me true love and happiness and that deeper connection to my own soul that I craved.

I had forgotten the truth of who I was. And worse—I hadn't even left room for any other possibility.

Where Is Your Energy?

Have you ever driven your car home and once there, realized that you had no memory of your drive home? How many times have you done something on autopilot, only to realize—with some degree of unease—that you can't even recall where your attention was while we were doing it?

That's how the majority of people spend their life—on autopilot and lost in thought-loops. They spend most of their lives in an unconscious state, in the in-between worlds where most of their energy, attention, and awareness is held practically hostage by their to-do lists and anxieties.

Without knowing where your awareness is in real time, your energy dissipates without you realizing it and you lose momentum on where to direct it. You end up scattered.

Here's an example of what I mean: Imagine having a conversation with someone, but you can sense that they aren't really listening to you. This happens all the time. All it takes is just one look into their eyes, and you notice that their consciousness is lost in an ocean of their own thoughts and stories. And if you look closely enough, you can even see that their energy isn't really in their body— they are not engaged in the conversation, verbally or nonverbally. They can't even digest what you're saying fully becausethey are not actually "home." This is what it's like to be around people who are not present.

My question is, if you're not embodied and present, then *who* is actually in control of your life? Your subconscious? The autopilot command center of your brain that only performs the same habits we are perpetually lost in? For most of us, the answer is certainly not the *conscious*version of you.

Most people live their waking hours on autopilot, always thinking about something in the future that will create happinessfor them or revisiting a time in their past. Some people skew more heavily into the future, while others fall more into melancholia of the past.

Unless we have a job that is aligned with our goals, interests, and values that is capable of *giving* us energy— which, let's be real, is a rarity these days—our jobs can energetically drain us, making it easier for us to be susceptible to rumination, exhaustion, and depletion. We may think work means sitting in front of a screen or showing up to an office to get paid, but that doesn't actually mean we're actively "working." During the 2008 financial crisis in NYC, when there was very little work happening at my company, many people reported feeling "exhausted" just sitting in front of their screen spending about half of their day on YouTube. I remember someone telling me they had watched every Korean soap opera available online at the time while working at a big corporate company and had run out of content, which led to an even more exhausting day for him. You may well roll your eyes at this, but distractions to kill time often do little to actually benefit us.

Speaking of, distractions are everywhere these days, and our job is to maintain our conscious hold on our free will and imagination. In a world that is fighting for our attention through every song, film, and ad—we can't take our awareness, what little we do have when not fully embodied and in control of our power, for granted. And when you lose track of your awareness, you might end up wondering where your life went and where the time went.

One of the very first principles I learned when I was studying energy was grounding. *Grounding* (often called "earthing" in modern complementary-health literature) isn't new: Cultures and healing traditions have long recommended direct contact with the earth—like walking barefoot, immersion in water, and other earth-based rituals—as a means to restore balance to the physical body.

Dr. Francesca McCartney, founder of the Academy of Intuition Medicine and a pioneer in energy medicine, describes grounding as a fundamental practice that involves the process of energetically aligning and connecting with the Earth's electromagnetic field. She emphasizes grounding as a fundamental practice for connecting one's energy to the Earth and living in the present moment, allowing us to truly listen to the world around us and direct our energy to where we want it to move. In her book, *Intuition Medicine: The Science of Energy*, she notes that grounding enables individuals to navigate the world with ease and grace, enhancing intuitive abilities and overall well-being.

To give you an initial idea of what a grounding practice might look like, this is what Dr. McCartney's program taught me: Take a seat and get comfortable, outside on the ground if possible. Visualize a cord extending from the base of your spine all the way into the Earth's core, imagining yourself connecting with the center of the Earth, which I picture as the womb of the planet. This imagery supports the exchange of energy between you and the

Earth, helping to harmonize and replenish your energy system.

Once you learn how to ground, the first thing you'll notice is how much more energy you have in your day to day experience. I don't just mean this spiritually; there is real evidence behind this practice. Both our bodies and the earth are literally electrically conductive and that electrical current can be transferred between us and the earth when we are in contact with it. Have you ever walked barefoot on the earth in nature or in the sand on a beach while on vacation? Did you notice how safe and connected you felt to the earth and to the present moment? According to an article in the *Journal of Inflammation Research*, contact between the human body and the Earth's surface causes many beneficial effects on the body, such as reducing pain and inflammation, healing quicker, strengthening the body's immune response, and "the prevention and treatment of chronic inflammatory and autoimmune diseases." This supports the idea that grounding boosts the immune system and healing processes at a biochemical level.

During an early interview on my podcast, I spoke with Step Sinatra, co-founder of Grounded.com, who told me of other health benefits that come from grounding, like regulating sleep, reducing stress and anxiety, improving circulation, increasing energy, and more. While the research is not yet comprehensive, it doesn't take a scientist or a doctor to notice that our bodies love being bathed in and connected to the earth.

In his book *Get Grounded, Get Well*, Sinatra also points out that we are the only species on Earth that does not sleep directly on the earth every single day, instead sleeping on elevated beds. We also do not remain physically connected to the Earth throughout the day—we usually wear shoes and spend most of our time indoors. As a result, we lose the energetic exchange that naturally occurs between the body and the Earth's electromagnetic field. Obviously, this is to our detriment, not only physically but mentally and spiritually as well.

Grounding to Become Present

We are not often present in the here and now because our mind likes to find a past or future moment that feels more alive or energetic. It is usually just a projection of a memory from the past or dream of the future and is often dissociative from whatever present feeling we're trying to avoid.

When I used to work in the corporate world, I would often ruminate about the future. One specific time, I remember sitting at the office thinking about my future vacation in Japan, then I looked at the clock and realized it was time for my next meeting. (Why do calendars only provide meeting options in thirty-minute chunks? I spent half the day in agenda-less meetings that probably could have ended much sooner than the thirty-allotted minutes or, even worse, the dreaded sixty minutes.)

I wasted so much time disassociating and ruminating about times of my life—because I'm a screenwriter, I like to think of these as "film frames"—other than the one I was in. Note that there is a difference between daydreaming, disassociating, and imagining intentionally.

Now, back to my ruminations about Japan while I was at my company's office in San Francisco. Even though I was physically in the office, my mind wanted to be almost anywhere else. That's why we feel depleted — because our life force, our "main character energy," is scattered across alternate stories instead of concentrated in the one we're actually living. The gas in the engine is given away to another car and another driver. I remember constantly feeling exhausted by the end of each day and had very little time for anything else beyond a few social interactions and workouts during the week.

So before we can actually manifest anything, we actually have to be here, *now*; we have to be embodied and grounded. Embodiment is the first step to creation. You can't write the story of your life as the main character if you're not in the scene.

How Grounding Nearly Saved My Life

Two years ago, I called a ride share car to take me to the San Francisco airport. Right before I requested the car, I had an intuitive sense that I should wait, but I shrugged it off.

When I got in the car, I sensed that the driver's energy felt ungrounded, but again, I shrugged it off. Wanting to soothe myself, I started to meditate and ground myself.

Ignoring my intuition that day almost cost me my life.

As we drove down US Route 101 in San Francisco, my eyes were closed and I was in a deep meditative state, grounding both myself and the car. About fifteen minutes into our drive, I heard the driver yell out "Holy shit!" and then, going seventy miles an hour, we slammed directly into a three-car pileup. Instantly, another car smashed into us from behind and my body flew in the air like a ping-pong ball.

I believe that because I was grounding myself and the car through meditation, I survived this horrific crash. Even the police and EMTs who came to examine the scene were dumbfounded, finding a smashed car with its air bags out and me in the backseat, still alive. Miraculously, my driver, while he was unconscious at the time, also made it out alive.

I'm curious how many other people's lives would change if they just started to practice grounding every day.

Learning how to ground and stay grounded throughout the day has been one of the most challenging energy exercises to master for me—and one of the most rewarding. When I was learning how to ground, I kept thinking that I had it, and yet months later, I realized that I was still barely grounding myself. It feels like the western world is filled with distractions that are tempting us to disconnect from the present moment: from doomscrolling and social media to netflix binges, not to mention conversations with other people who are mostly ungrounded themselves.

Before I understood grounding, my attention and energy was often scattered. I used to spend most of my days on the phone, on the computer, and on a screen watching a show or a movie. In order to remain neutral, I learned to keep my attention in the center of my head, so I could access my subconscious.

Putting Your Awareness in the Hypothalamus

In her empirical work and teachings, Dr. Francesca McCartney describes putting your awareness in the "center of your head" in the hypothalamus and then deliberately raising that frequency as a way to access and transmit healing energy. In this space, we are using a practical image to move attention out of the thinking prefrontal cortex mind and into a deep, regulatory center.

Literally, the hypothalamus is a deep brain structure that organizes hormones, sleep, appetite, and autonomic state. Metaphorically and practically, this instruction means: *Shift your felt-attention into the body's center of regulation*, so the nervous system can rebalance and you can act from embodied clarity rather than prefrontal cortex rumination.

This shift is a skillful shorthand: By focusing interoceptive attention on the center of your head, you can change signals to and from the hypothalamus, vagus, and other autonomic circuits, which produces measurable calming and clarity in practice.

Now, with all of this information, let's explore *how* to ground.

Reclaiming Your Energy Through Grounding

Have you ever noticed how you feel when you connect to the earth? There is a shift, a settling; a sense of returning to yourself.

To move our energy upward into creativity and higher consciousness, we must first root it in the present moment. Expansion requires grounding, because without a stable foundation, elevated states can't fully anchor into reality. Grounding exercises often use the analogy of being hugged and protected by Mother Earth, and for good reason. Like all the physiological benefits that come with being grounded that were listed earlier in this chapter, being grounded gives our body a feeling of safety and security. The body must feel safe to explore new ideas, to open to inspiration, and to translate higher visions into form. When we reclaim our energy from the past and root it in now, our creative power becomes both inspired and embodied. It also feels good mentally and spiritually to give your fear and worry to the Earth, allowing the Earth to transmute that energy so that you can fill your being with her energy of unconditional love.

Ritual: How to Ground Yourself

Without further ado, here is a grounding meditation that you can try when you are feeling anxious, disconnected, or stressed, or whenever you need to feel a bit more calm:

1. Sit or stand comfortably with both feet on the floor.
2. Let your shoulders soften. Place one hand over your belly and one hand over your heart, or simply rest your hands on your thighs.
3. Close your eyes. (Pause for three seconds.)
4. Take three slow breaths: in for four seconds, out for six seconds, letting each exhale relax you further. (Pause for six seconds.)

5. Bring your attention to the soles of your feet. Feel their weight, the pressure from where they rest against the floor, and their temperature—the sense of connection with what you're standing on. Imagine soft, steady roots extending from the base of your spine going down to the center of the earth. (Pause for eight seconds.)

6. Visualize these roots reaching down through soil, rock, and the layers of the earth. See them go deeper— through rivers of mineral and warm core—until they reach the very center of the Earth. (Pause for eight seconds.)

7. At the center, imagine a warm, receptive field—a place that gathers and holds energy. Imagine gravity pulling you downward.

8. Now, gently gather a column of earth energy up from that center into your roots and let it rise into your feet. Notice the sensation as it fills your legs with solid, steady support. (Pause for ten seconds.)

9. Slowly draw that earth energy up into your pelvis, your belly, into the space behind the sternum, and finally into the small, quiet center in the middle of your head—the soft listening place in the midline. Allow the energy to settle there like a calm, golden pebble. (Pause for ten seconds.)

10. Breathe into that center for ten slow breaths (in for four seconds, out for six seconds)—each breath deepening the feeling of being rooted and contained. With each exhale, allow tension to drop deeper into the earth.

11. Now make a gentle circuit: Imagine a luminous thread running from that inner center, down through your body, out your roots, into the center of the Earth, and back up again. Feel the steady two-way flow: sending, receiving, and settling. (Pause for ten seconds.)

12. Take one more deep, nourishing breath. Open your eyes slowly and go about your day, practicing this exercise whenever you need to.

Well, were you able to visualize this meditation? Do you feel more calm and safe in your body?

Before I learned how to ground, I had a number of creative ideas that went nowhere, because I didn't know how to move and transform my energy. So, I spent a number of years researching what activities and frameworks best help people become more grounded and came up with this list. If you can't become grounded in your internal world through a visualization meditation like the one above, here are eight other ways to find help from the outside world to become grounded. When I was learning how to ground myself, it took me over nine months of daily meditation and practice to feel safe and relaxed in my physical body. Over time, it became habitual. These eight exercises are meant to be practically applied to your life, so try them out in moments when you feel anxious or your energy feels scattered and see what works for you.

1. Anchor Yourself in Time and Space

One relatively easy way to become more grounded is to orient yourself in the present moment. Begin by placing your hand on your heart, closing your eyes, and taking a deep breath. Then, state your name out loud to yourself, followed by the date, the time, and the city you are in. Then take another deep breath.

This exercise has an almost immediate effect and helps you ground into the present moment. It acts as a reset button whenever you need it.

2. Ask Yourself: Where Is My Awareness Right Now?

Your awareness is constantly shifting, like a camera lens adjusting its focus. However, most people do not consciously choose where their attention goes.

A powerful way to bring yourself back to the present moment is by asking, *Where is my awareness right now?*

By posing this question, you disrupt autopilot mode; you snap out of unconscious thinking patterns and regain control of your attention. This practice allows you to observe your thoughts rather than being controlled by them.

So where is your awareness right now? Where are you placing your attention?

You can also take it a step farther by asking yourself: *Where do I wish my awareness to be right now?*

3. Physically Touch the Earth

Direct contact with the Earth is one of the easiest and most effective ways to ground yourself. Walking barefoot on grass, soil, or sand helps regulate the nervous system and restore balance to the body. If it's winter and there's only snow around, then at least go out and spend a moment touching the snow with your hands.

If you don't have nature nearby, if you're in the city for example, you can even touch a tree or a plant as a start. The key is to touch Mother Earth in some way every single day.

4. Immerse Yourself in Water

Water is a natural conductor of energy, which makes it a powerful tool for grounding. Physically touching, dipping your feet in, or swimming in a natural body of water such as the ocean, a lake, a river, or a stream is very grounding. Immersing yourself in water is a reminder that you are in a body and not a floating consciousness or mind, helping to bring your awareness back to your center as well as connecting you to the natural world.

If you don't live by body of water, even a simple shower and a warm bath, especially with epsom salts, have the same effect. Have you ever noticed how different you feel after a shower? It can literally and physically serve as a reset from your previous energy state to a new one.

5. Yoga Nidra and Body Scanning

I first learned about yoga nidra in Bali at a yoga retreat and found it to be an excellent gateway to return back to your body. Essentially, yoga nidra is a body scan practice in which a speaker will guide you through parts of the body, and your energy and consciousness will move your awareness to each of those body parts in turn. Inducing a state between wakefulness and sleep and facilitating profound relaxation and self-awareness, yoga nidra allows you to be acutely aware of your body and "fill your body" with your awareness and consciousness. This practice can be done at any part of the day.

The science behind this practice clearly shows numerous physical and mental benefits. A 2023 pilot study in *PLOS ONE* found that after just two weeks of twenty-minute daily yoga nidra sessions, participants experienced increased deep sleep efficiency and enhanced cognitive functions, including better memory and decision-making.

Bringing awareness to the body through a structured body scan like with yoga nidra can be a powerful way to reintegrate scattered energy and return to a state of balance.

6. Sound Therapy & Binaural Beats

Sound has a profound effect on our nervous systems. Certain frequencies can induce a state of calm and balance, helping to bring your awareness to the present moment. Even listening to one song can immediately shift you into a different state of consciousness.

I had the opportunity to interview Elizabeth Krasnoff, PhD, a researcher in the field of sound therapy and binaural beats, on my podcast. She explained that binaural beats can balance and synchronize the right and left hemispheres of your brain, and this synchronization promotes relaxation, focus, and a deeper connection to both body and mind. Hemi-Sync, one of the most well-known companies in this field, and many other artists specifically create binaural beats for this purpose. Try listening to them. If you have difficulty grounding through some of the other physical practices listed here, sound therapy might be the gateway you need.

7. Scent Therapy for Grounding

Create a grounded atmosphere in your home with the scents of nature like cedar, pine, palo santo, sage, sandalwood, and cinnamon.

These scents and others have an immediate calming effect on the nervous system. Filling your space with grounding aromas through candles, incense, or diffusers can help create an environment that supports presence.

8. Balance Yin and Yang Energies with Qigong

Qigong is an ancient mind-body practice that combines breath work, movement, and meditation to cultivate balanced energy. The National Qigong Association defines it as a "system that integrates posture, breathing techniques, and focused intent to improve mental and physical health." I personally enjoy practicing Qigong with Thomas Droge, who also joined me on my *Gateways to Awakening* podcast to share his philosophy on this ancient art. His teachings include many beautiful practices that help you connect with the earth and ground your energy into the present moment.

Further, we can add both masculine and feminine movement practices in our daily practice. In my podcast interview with Beth Riley, we spoke about the masculine nature of the way we move in the western world—from aerobics to running and to basketball to football, which often have very linear and force-driven movements. Qigong focuses on more circular, feminine non-linear, and fluid movements that tend to calm the nervous system and balance and harmonize our feminine (yin) and masculine (yang) energies.

9. Create Space for Silence and Stillness

In a world that constantly demands our attention, silence has become a rare and powerful tool. Many people associate silence with formal meditation retreats, such as Vipassana, where participants spend ten days in complete silence. However, you do not need to escape to a monastery to integrate silence into your life. Personally, when embracing silence, I realized that all the subtle cues—like a visual, a felt knowing, a contraction, an expansion, a particular taste in my mouth, a picture in my head, or a clear knowing—I was told to ignore for the sake of logic were actually preventing me from making better choices and decisions rather than helping me.

I recommend beginning with one hour of silence each day — no phone, no distractions, no external noise. If you can't find a quiet space indoors, even sitting in your car or garage works. The purpose is simply to create space for yourself and to sit, breathe, and allow your thoughts and emotions to surface and settle.

Some people prefer walking in silence, and that can be powerful too. But in my experience, there's something uniquely transformative about sitting in stillness and allowing yourself to be fully present with whatever arises.

I find that this is the most difficult of tasks for most people who are so used to numbing themselves whenever there is a dull or uncomfortable moment. But when we remove external stimulation, we allow the mind to slow down, the body to reset, and the subconscious to better integrate thoughts and emotions.

Integration and Wholeness

To be human is to feel a separation from the whole. We are born into a body, into form, into individuality. From the moment we arrive, we long for something we can't quite name: A sense of belonging. A return to something vast, something infinite and bigger.

An important part of being grounded and embodied is the feeling of integration and wholeness.

Many of us walk through life unconscious about that hole inside of us, and instead of looking inward, we search for that wholeness outside ourselves. We chase it through validation, relationships, and material success. We build lives around the hole, hoping that something out there will fill the empty space we feel inside.

Yet, the truth is—we were never separate to begin with.

We all come from a universal Source, and we will all return to that same universal Source someday. To be a soul in a human body is an experience of fragmentation, especially with our body's limited five senses of perception. We must remind ourselves, every day, that even though we may not physically be connected to that wholeness on a spiritual level, we are still always connected to the world around us.

Grounding can help us feel whole and integrated with all that is.

The greatest dis-ease of our time isn't physical—it's a disconnection from self. Imagine yourself on a boat in the ocean: All of your energy exists on that boat, protecting it from water leaking in. Every time we give our attention away and believe we are separate from the world around us, a bit of our energy dissipates, carried off by the wind, and our boat springs a leak. Over time, we're stuck in the middle of the ocean without any sense of agency or direction on a sinking boat.

To be able to wield your energy and direct it like a great magician or wizard, you must collect it first in this present moment. Once you're grounded, embodied, and integrated, we can move on to the next of the ten energy mastery codes, which focuses on lowering the assigned importance we place on people and things in our lives and choosing to live your life with levity.

CHAPTER 3

Code #3: Levity, Letting Go, and Being Open to Receive

When things get too serious, you're moving in the wrong direction.

—Frederick Dodson

During Neo's training sessions with Morpheus in *The Matrix*, Morpheus never stresses, never forces, and never panics—he moves effortlessly, as if he already knows the outcome. Neo, on the other hand, is intense, rigid, and trying too hard. He doubts himself, second-guesses his abilities, and overthinks every move. But the moment Neo lets go, the moment he stops making it so *important*, everything shifts.

This is the paradox: The less you grip the world, the more power you have over it. The moment you stop needing something to happen, you remove the resistance that was blocking it in the first place. Morpheus embodies this principle—he moves with certainty but never clings. He leads with levity and, in doing so, becomes unstoppable.

This chapter will delve into the levels of importance that we often assign to people, relationships, places, jobs, and many more things in our lives and how this can often hold us back. We'll also look at how choosing to let go and embracing a more neutral state of balance can actually make space for and invite what you want in your life rather than forcing it to. Lastly, we'll discuss how leading a life of levity and infusing humor into difficult moments can lessen unnecessary frustration and make your life lighter, allowing you to enjoy it more fully.

The Cost of Holding on Too Tightly

There was a time in my life when I felt like I was constantly getting struck by calamity and drama. I was full of creative but anxious energy and was obsessed with finding ways to express myself and my ideas, but they often came with a cost. It seemed like one thing after another was slipping away from me, leaving me depleted after what was supposed to be a big win.

Looking back now, I see how I was unconsciously feeding this cycle, chasing drama to justify why things were happening to me rather than looking at how exactly I was attempting to accomplish my goals. It was only when I took a step back to pause and reflect on my inner state and drop my labels of importance on what I was doing did everything change.

Anytime we create a hierarchy between ourselves and another person, place, idea, or thing—imbuing the relationship, goal, or concept with an "importance"—we distort the energy around us and it. And the Universe always comes to collect on the energetic debt we take out, eager to restore balance. When that correction comes, it often arrives through the shadow—forcing balance in ways you might not expect or want.

I've seen this pattern everywhere and have observed people encourage each other to create importance around people and situations in their life. Many friendships and relationships are built on a shared sense of complaining and victimhood, such as how gossiping can lead to the judgement and vilification of others, fueling conflict and anxiety in both parties. Some people, not knowing how to generate their own energy, even destabilize others just to extract energy from them. These people are sometimes known as "energy vampires." According to self-help guru and motivational speaker Jim Rohn, we are often an accumulation and average of the five people we spend the most time with, so our shared complaints, conflicts, and anxieties only reinforce our sense of victimization, leaving all those involved depleted and drained.

This is precisely why drama often comes as a domino effect. One day, you're happy and calm, and the next, it seems like you're sliding into an abyss of chaos. Your mind starts to spin, and suddenly, you're not sure what happened. It doesn't help that drama often follows groups of people and friend circles as well, emphasizing the idea that we all feed off of each other's energies, whether good or bad.

What you put out into the world comes back to you in equal measure. Negativity only invites more negativity. If you find yourself in unhealthy friendships, relationships, or situations, consider what sort of energy you're putting into it—is it at all similar to what you're receiving?

This concept reminds me of what Maureen St. Germain spoke about in a workshop I attended: You should only tell your sad story three times. Why three times? Because it allows you to process it and then turn it into a gift. Anything beyond three times is actually reinforcing the neural network of victimhood, and energetically, you are inviting more of those stories you don't want in your life to repeat. Telling your story once allows you to release it. Telling it twice lets you reflect and gain perspective. Telling it three times turns it into wisdom—a gift that can help others. Anything beyond that only creates a hierarchy of importance that is unnecessary and creates an imbalance of energy that will bring unexpected consequences to your life.

One summer, after a breakup that left me feeling lost, I kept hearing this phrase: "Don't worship false gods." This is a biblical phrase, and in a religious context, it warns against idolizing material things, power, or false deities or people over oneself. It was a clear instruction not to place my old partner or any relationship on any kind of pedestal.

Now, looking back on that moment, I laugh, because I essentially practiced the opposite of this code back then. In many cultures, we're conditioned to idolize people and assign them a significance they were never meant to carry. But that weight is never good for them—and it's certainly not good for us. We only end up energetically rejecting and polarizing the people that we cling and attach to. You can care for and value people deeply without making them more important than yourself.

I have a friend who has been single for over seven years and longs for a deep romantic connection. Yet, every time she meets someone new, she floods the relationship with an almost otherworldly and fantastical intensity—placing the new love interest on a pedestal and elevating them before their relationship even has a chance to grow naturally. In doing so, she loses herself in the process, making the guy and the relationship more important than anything else—including her own sense of self. This just goes to show that when you overinflate the significance of a person, place, or thing, you create an energetic imbalance. Like two particles trying to occupy the same space, the dynamic becomes unsustainable, and the very attachment my friend desires ends up pushing the other person away.

This is true not just for elevating someone's or something's importance but also for lowering your own importance compared to another's. No person, place, or thing is any more or less worthy than you. If you place a greater importance on either yourself or someone else, then you will inevitably push them away from you. In order to retain your own energetic balance and not fall prey to pedestalization—either your own or someone else's—you must be mindful of maintaining a sense of neutrality and heart-centeredness when you're in the company of others.

No one is better than you, and nor are you better than anyone else.

A State of Balance

Managing your attachments and the level of importance you place on people, situations, and other energies is one of the most important concepts to master when attempting to follow the third energy mastery code. Life is built on polarity—positive and negative forces in constant interplay. When you remain centered between these forces, you create balance, allowing energy to flow steadily rather than fluctuating between extremes. True connection, whether in love or life, comes from this equilibrium.

All energy systems are naturally drawn to return to a state of balance—a state of neutrality.

You will notice when you have created distortion in your energy states of pedestalization and subjugation becauseyour external reality will let you know. In order to restore equilibrium, this displaced energy will seek to influence other areas in your life to compensate for the imbalance. The unresolved energetic distortion doesn't just disappear—it finds another outlet, manifesting in unexpected ways to restore wholeness.

Balance is key.

So, how do we balance value without tipping into over-importance? Let's break it down.

Think about it like this: Have you ever clicked on a button, link, or app on your phone or computer over and over until, at some point, it freezes, crashes, or becomes unresponsive? Something similar happens when we hyperfocus on a specific aspect of our lives: We overload the system with too much attention, too much effort, too much importance—and suddenly, things stop working.

In comparison, if we let go of that hyperfocus, that level of importance that we have given to the situation, and remain in balance—or, to keep with the technology analogy above, we click only once and wait for our device to load—then we allow the natural flow of energy to continue.

One example that helped me understand this recently was when I drove into San Francisco for a birthday party and left my car on an unsafe street in the Mission district. As soon as I got out of my car, another person who had just been dropped off by an Uber exclaimed, "You're just going to leave your car there?"

She proceeded to walk with me to the party entrance, recounting all her horrific stories of car break-ins and how dramatic the experiences had been. I could feel her nervous and somewhat neurotic energy, and I sensed how she was projecting her fear into my energetic field.

I decided that I would drop the importance I was beginning to place on the situation, but I could still feel my energy slightly weakened by her fear. San Francisco *is* a city known for its high rates of car break-in.

At the party, I occasionally wondered throughout the evening if my car was okay. This was not a thought that I ever normally entertain. Thoughts, just like energy, can either be invested or spent. I often assume the best is always happening in my life, rather than being concerned about things that haven't happened.

Five hours later, I walked back to my car and found it still there, fully intact.

Phew.

I thought I had dodged the fearful, nervous energy brought on by my earlier interaction and proceeded to drive home, singing mantras to myself. Since I was new to Mill Valley, which is in the North Bay area, I was also unfamiliar with the street signs and the neighborhood.

As I exited the highway at high speed, I accidentally drove through a stop sign. Luckily, not a single car was in sight—it was late, and Mill Valley is known for early nights. As I abruptly stopped after realizing I had driven through the sign, I hesitated for a moment before continuing to drive.

Suddenly, a police car appeared behind me.

I stopped and pulled over.

The officer asked, "Have you been drinking?"

I replied, "No, I don't drink." Then I admitted, "I know what I did. I'm just new to the area, and I completely missed the sign."

She asked for my driver's license and registration.

Sighing, I decided to drop the level of importance I was instinctually putting on this situation and let it be okay if I did get a ticket. I also sent the officer loving energy and appreciation. I let go completely of the situation.

A few minutes later, the officer returned and said, "I'm going to give you a warning this time."

This is an example of dropping importance and attachment. The older version of me would have tightened up, and I was tempted to do so at first, clenching my energy instead of being in a state of openness and flow.

The Danger of Assigning Exaggerated Importance

One of the biggest traps we fall into—whether in work, relationships, or life in general—is overloading situations with too much importance and clinginess. When we attach excessive significance to something, we create tension, resistance, and often, unnecessary stress. The truth is that most things in life are valuable but very few are truly "important." We also need to stay in a balanced state to live a life that is easy and relaxed and calm. Mania is not a necessary—or enjoyable—state to live life.

Your reaction to life affects your life. If you make things into a big deal with the way you respond to them, then they will be.

Here are a few common examples I often hear about: The relationship you overanalyze falls apart; the job you obsess over becomes overwhelming; the project you over-engineer loses its magic. Just like the example of over-clicking on your device, instead, step back. Reduce its importance and let go. Things tend to flow better when we stop trying to force them.

Even if the "worst" thing in the world happens to you, whatever meaning you assign to it is your decision. You can decide if it is the "worst" thing ever, or you can decide it is the "best" thing. Your belief about what's happened will often create a cocktail of emotions, thoughts, and feelings. It will then take you into different frequency states and outcomes.

I know it's difficult to change one's reactions to situations when in the moment, they feel so incredibly life-changing. Here's an example: Let's say you go through a breakup with someone that you loved very much. You could assign varying degrees of meaning, such as:

- I'm never going to find a person like this again. They were the love of my life.
- I'm heartbroken and can hardly move out of bed. I know it's been years, but I still cannot trust another partner in my life.

- Perhaps the Universe has someone even better in mind for me, and I need to let go of this person in order for us to find each other.

- Wow, I love all the new ways I'm able to spend my time, all the people I'm meeting, and all the new hobbies I've picked up.

- Energy has restructured itself in my life.

- I feel deeply connected to the Universe and walk through life with a sense of certainty and wholeness.

What about if it were a different situation? Here are some other examples of exaggerated importance levels: The executive who thinks they're more important than their team: likely disconnected. The person who worships their relationship: likely suffocating it. The entrepreneur obsessed with their startup company: likely burning out. No matter what the situation, the lesson is clear: Assigning too much importance to something will only create hardship because you are attempting to force the situation rather than letting it go and adopting neutrality.

This is not to say that you must not *care* about what is happening in your life. For example, you can love deeply without making someone the center of your Universe. You can care about work without making it a life-or-death matter. You can pursue success without feeling like the world will end if you fail. When you keep things in proper proportion, you move with flow, not force.

Energy Wants to Be in Balance

This applies to everything—business deals, personal challenges, even spiritual growth. If you're not laughing and enjoying yourself, you're likely off track.

A sense of humor neutralizes resistance and brings life into balance. It shifts you from tension (low-energy contraction) to ease (high-energy expansion). Think about people who handle challenges with lightness—they radiate an effortless kind of mastery.

If you're in a difficult situation, ask yourself: *Can I find humor in this?* If the answer is no, you're probably taking it too seriously. Oftentimes, we forget that life is impermanent. You can also ask yourself this question: *Will this matter in one hundred years?*

If you're feeling stuck, frustrated, or that things aren't working—try to inject fun into the situation.

Play. Experiment. Let go. Ask yourself, *How could this situation become humorous? How could I find some lightness in this moment?*

After interviewing more than 250 leaders in the world of consciousness, I've realized that the highest form of consciousness is to have a sense of humor and to be able to accept a paradoxical approach.

Some of you may object to this, asking, "Isn't humor a spiritual bypass?"

No, humor is the macro lens view on the thing you're upset about. This perspective is not spiritual bypassing because it doesn't deny, suppress, or invalidate difficult emotions—it reframes them through a wider lens of awareness. In contrast, humor and the ability to hold paradox demonstrate a high level of consciousness by integrating both the gravity of a situation and the levity that comes from seeing its broader context.

Humor, when used consciously, is a tool to gain perspective, not a means to escape discomfort. It allows you to see the absurdity of rigid attachments rather than running away from them. True consciousness embraces contradictions: light and dark, pain and joy, suffering and wisdom. Humor is the recognition that life is complex and paradoxical—not black and white.

Some of the wisest spiritual leaders—like the Dalai Lama, Ram Dass, and even Zen masters—infuse humor into their teachings. Why? Becausewhen you're deeply in tune with life, you realize that seriousness is often self-imposed.

When you laugh at something, it doesn't mean you're denying its difficulty—it means you've elevated yourself beyond its ability to control you. Humor is not about dismissing reality; it's about seeing reality from a higher state of awareness.

Ritual: Practicing Letting Go

Here are some ideas to change your idea of work to play and inject levity into your life:

- Make your workday a game.
- Treat failures like funny plot twists in a movie.
- Ask yourself, *If this werea sitcom, how would this sceneplay out?*
- Try something different every day for at least twenty-one days.

Here are some questions that you could journal about or simply ask yourself:

- What are you making too important today?
- What are you attached to?
- What are some of the ways you can let go of attachment and importance about your current life?
- How can you see situations from a space of humor instead?

Nothing is truly important. It might be valuable, but it's not necessarily important.

The best performers in any field—athletes, artists, business leaders—get this. They show up, they do the work, but they're not strangling the outcome with attachment. They know that pressure kills performance.

Next time you feel stress creeping in, ask yourself: *If I took a step back and looked at this situation from an unemotional perspective, how much would this matter?* Most of the time, you'll realize it doesn't. The lighter you hold things, the easier and faster they move. The moment you make something too important, it controls *you* instead of *you* controlling it. Life isn't meant to be a rigid, high-stakes chess game. It's meant to be a dance.

Life is inherently humorous *because* it's a paradox. We make plans, set goals, and strategize, only for life to throw in a plot twist that no one saw coming. It's as if the Universe is a prankster that delights in reminding us that control is just an illusion. We take ourselves so seriously, and our egos believe we are at the center of the Universe, but life has a way of humbling us with misplaced coffee cups, autocorrect disasters, and more.

Main Character Energy isn't about control; it's about **presence**. It's knowing that you are the lead in your life's story, but also that the plot is alive and improvisational. The main character doesn't cling to the script—they dance with it. Levity, then, is the soul of Main Character Energy: the ability to laugh at your own seriousness, to find beauty in absurdity, and to surrender to the unknown with grace.

Life moves forward whether we're ready or not. Whether we "have time" or not. One day we're young and invincible, and the next we're excited about good parking spots and early bedtime. Time's relentless progression is both tragic and hilarious.

We are sentient beings flying through an infinite Universe on a blue and green dot. We are made up of stardust, communicating through vibrations, noises, and symbols. This in itself is both profound and absolutely ridiculous.

There is a difference between the serious versus the sacred. Many people conflate being serious with being sacred, but they are actually fundamentally different states of consciousness. The serious is heavy, rigid, and often rooted in fear or ego, while the sacred is expansive, light, and infused with deep reverence.

As for my friend who was longing to find a romantic partner, she still finds herself in the same pattern—falling hard, attaching deeply like a love addict, and ultimately watching each relationship slip away. The cycle continues because the energy she brings into love is one of scarcity, urgency, and pedestalization.

The lesson remains: What you want in life is not something to grasp or chase. It's something to allow, to flow with, to meet on equal ground.

The moment we make something *too* important, we create resistance. But when we relax into our own wholeness, relationships become a reflection of that—not a desperate attempt to complete something we believe is missing.

So the question isn't *when* she'll find love, but *how* she'll shift her energy to allow it to find her.

The Key to Getting Everything You Want

The paradox of life is this: The more attached you are to an outcome, the more resistance you create. The moment you grip too tightly, you block energy's natural flow.

Most people operate from a place of attachment. They obsess over the *how* and *when*, constantly searching for what's wrong instead of reinforcing what's right. They're desperate for a result, and that desperation signals lack. And lack only attracts more lack.

The real secret is to commit fully but detach from the outcome. Be *all in* on your vision but unmoved by temporary setbacks. Show up with certainty but be sure you don't need things to unfold in a specific way. Instead of looking for what's missing, train your brain to look for what's already working—because whatever you focus on expands.

J. Krishnamurti once said, "I don't mind what happens." This is the ultimate state of power—where you take inspired action but remain unshaken by the outcome. When you stop needing it, it comes faster. When you surrender, you create space for something even bigger than what you imagined.

We came here to play. To enjoy life. To let go.

And the moment you do, everything comes rushing in.

So the real question is this: Can you commit without attachment and enjoy the unfolding? Can you hold the pen lightly and let the story surprise you? Because that's where the real magic of life happens— where the main character is laughing along with the Universe. Next, we look at another seemingly magical concept: Code #4, which focuses on the power of belief and how the Universe will agree with whatever you believe.

CHAPTER 4

Code #4: What You Identify With, You Become

Environment is stronger than will—but your energy and awareness can change your environment.

—Paramahansa Yogananda

In one of the scenes of *The Matrix*, a little boy tells Neo, "There is no spoon.…It is not the spoon that bends, it is only yourself."

The young boy is teaching Neo about belief and self-concept. If you see yourself as limited, weak, and incapable of bending a spoon, the world will reflect those constraints back to you. Similarly, when Neo chose to *believe* that he was The One, he shifted into the state in which he *was* The One.

This chapter on the fourth energy mastery code is all about examining how you walk through life, the difference between your identity and your self-concept, and how when you shift your self-concept—when you see yourself as powerful, limitless, and adaptable—your external reality will reflect that accordingly. True transformation is about changing who you believe yourself to be at the deepest level. For when your identity shifts, so does everything around you.

Offense vs. Defense

I believe each of us is watching in real time our own film reel that we call life. This film reel is a projection of our life experience shaped by our energy, past experiences, cultural conditioning, and subconscious beliefs. This reel dictates the station we tune into, the patterns we repeat, and the reality we create.

Yet, most people live reactively. They wake up and react to the day. They react to the people they see, their morning routine, the news, and the conversations around them. They let external forces dictate their internal state.

The alternative model, which so few people are doing now, is to decide how they're going to feel and think for the day, and then start their day. To use a sports analogy, rather than playing "offense" in life, they are often playing "defense"—reacting to everything that the world throws at them.

What if, instead of playing defense—constantly responding to the world—you played offense, directing your energy with intention?

What would happen if you created a thought and feeling playbook—a strategic guide that outlines how to respond to each thought and feeling that comes up—for your day, week, or even your entire year? Instead of being swept up in your defensive reactions to social media, the news, workplace gossip, and other constant stimuli, you would be the one setting the tone. You would be able to take control of your life.

How Identity and Self-Concept Dictate Reality

Our identity is the collection of specific traits, roles, and labels that we use to define who we are, while our self-concept represents the sum of our beliefs, perceptions, values, and assumptions we hold about ourselves. Identity focuses on who you are in relation to the world, while self-concept focuses on how you see yourself, regardless of external validation. Identity is largely influenced by external factors, such as the roles we play in society (e.g.,

"I am a mother" and "I am an artist"), whereas self-concept is shaped more by internal beliefs (e.g., "I am confident" and "I am creative").

Your identity is the structure of who you are. Your self-concept is the lens through which you experience that identity. By intentionally shaping your self-concept, you can elevate your identity and step into a more empowered version of yourself.

Right now, you already have a self-concept. Many of you likely are not aware of the self-concept that you're projecting out into the world. A self-concept is the mental image or perception you have of yourself. It's how you define who you are, what you're capable of, and what's possible for you. Your self-concept influences your thoughts, behaviors, decisions, and ultimately, the reality you create.

Ritual: Exploring Your Self-Concept

If you want to know what your self-concept is, take a look at the life that you've created. Whatever you have surrounding you is usually in alignment with what you value and what you believe you deserve. Answer each item below in full sentences. Be honest; this is for you. Try journaling about your answers if you want. Say silently or aloud: "I am willing to see myself clearly. I meet myself with honesty, compassion, and curiosity."

- **Abundance vs. scarcity:** Do you feel abundance in your life or scarcity? Give two concrete examples that support your answer.
- **Beauty:** Do you have beauty surrounding you? Describe three details in your environment that feel beautiful to you right now.
- **Relationships and friendships:** What types of friendships and relationships do you have? Name two qualities you most often show in your close relationships (e.g., loyal, private, generous).
- **What you deserve:** What do you believe you deserve in work, love, money, and rest? Write one sentence for each domain.

Here is another ritual you can try. This is a quick rating and pattern check that you can do in your journal so you have enough room to write out your responses. For each of the dimensions below, write in your journal a score between 1 and 10 and then write one sentence explaining the score, with 1 being low, and 10 being high.

- Abundance
- Beauty in environment
- Creativity belief
- Relationship health

Is there a single pattern that you notice across these ratings? When you step back and look at the pattern, it often reveals the energetic story you've been telling about who you are and what you're worthy of. If you notice that certain areas feel lower or more constricted, pause and ask yourself why. What experiences or beliefs might be shaping that perception? Or if one area stands out as higher than the rest, what does that reveal about where you naturally allow energy and abundance to flow?

Your self-concept often suggests what you are comfortable receiving and what you believe you deserve. You're essentially telling the world, "I believe I am this," and the world will respond with "Okay, yes, you are," and show you evidence of your belief.

Your self-concept is built from:

- **Past experiences**—such as successes, failures, traumas, etc.

- **Cultural and societal programming**—such as family, religion, media, education, etc.
- **Beliefs about yourself**—usually formed in childhood and reinforced over time
- **Your identity labels**—such as "introvert," "leader," "artist," "athlete," "victim," etc.
- **Feedback from others**—what people have told you about yourself

Your self-concept acts as a blueprint, shaping both what you expect from life and what life expects from you. Once you have a self-concept, you unconsciously act in ways that reinforce it. For example:

- If you see yourself as a creative person, you'll naturally gravitate toward artistic opportunities and a creative career or life.
- If you believe you're bad at relationships, you'll self-sabotage or attract unhealthy dynamics and likely find partners who aren't good for you.
- If you identify as a leader, you'll instinctively take charge in situations and likely be rewarded in your career.

Think about it like this: What did people tell you about you when you were a child? Did they remark that you were "smart" or a "genius," or "dumb," or "beautiful," or "overweight"? What did you take in? What did you not take in?

Most people's self-concept was originally created based on what other people said about them. Over time, especially in adulthood, it is our responsibility to question those labels and decide if they are just a projection, said unconsciously at the time, or are, in fact, true.

Let me tell you a little story about how my self-concept came to be defined as I grew up. I came of age during the time of the first Nintendo games, and the main characters for one of the first games were, of course, Mario and Luigi. Now, for all those who grew up in a house as the youngest, you likely were told that you had to play Luigi, the subservient sidekick to Mario.

I went on to play Luigi for as long as I remember, after my early negotiations with my elder sibling proved to be fruitless. But I secretly wondered when I would eventually play Mario. I dreamed that one day, I would be "big" enough to play the lead.

From that day on, I began to act out of that identity: I would acquiesce, wait my turn, and follow rather than lead. Over time, those repeated actions and the feedback that I received "solidified" a Luigi-style self-concept: A present-tense belief about who I was that organized my attention, choice, and behavior.

Being the youngest in the room meant that I was taught, again and again, to take the supporting role. I learned early to step back, to be the friendly fixer, the one who kept the peace. Those small, repeated choices accumulated into a habit: I moved earlier into sidekick energy because that was the path of least resistance, the path that kept the family calm and earned me the easy praise of being "helpful."

That pattern was not just social theatre; it rewired the way I saw myself. Each time I accepted the Luigi role, I collected a little proof that I belonged in the background, so my brain stopped betting on me as the lead. I didn't need a dramatic failure to learn this; I learned it through the quiet rewards of cooperation and the absence of risk. The label of "youngest" became shorthand for available options, narrowing the range of choices I imagined for myself. Over time, the inner narrative stitched itself into identity—not because I was incapable, but because I had practiced being the one who *supports* instead of the one who *starts*. I was practicing the role of the supporting actor instead of the main character of my life.

And I'm sure my brother would argue that the opposite is also true. The eldest is usually handed the invisible clipboard of responsibility. That dynamic plays out often: The youngest gets extra attention, extra cuddles, and rescues from mistakes while the oldest is unconsciously nudged, and sometimes even deputized, to keep the household running. Medical and popular write-ups support this: Firstborns often receive more undivided parental attention early on, and that attention can translate into expectations of leadership and caretaking.

Notice how these micro-moments and the subtle nuance of being the youngest, oldest, or the middle-child all play a huge role in how we see ourselves later in life, our belief patterns about responsibility, and so much more. These tiny moments—the ones we brush off as "just childhood games"—shape us beyond measure. Whether you were the youngest, the oldest, the only, or the one in-between…your place in the family story becomes a template. It teaches you what to expect, what role you're "allowed" to play, who you're "supposed" to become, and what's required of you to finally be "big enough."

The story of Mario and Luigi is not just about a video game. It's about the subtle scripting of our self-concept—the unconscious belief systems that define whether we lead, follow, comply, or rise.

Neville Goddard, a teacher in the world of manifestation that I personally keep returning to, often spoke about the self-concept as the foundation of all reality creation. He says that you can only experience what you believe about yourself and that you cannot experience anything outside of your self-concept. In other words, you experience what you're comfortable receiving. This is actually good news, because that means when you change your self-concept, your life also changes, often quite dramatically.

Ritual: Self-ConceptInventory

You can decide to keep those old labels that you may not have even created for yourself, or you can create ones that feel more aligned. One practice I've leaned into for years is understanding the self-concept and identity I've built at any given moment in time. I regularly take an inventory of my self-concept and experiment with how I can show up differently—more intentionally, more aligned. My outer experience is often reflecting back to me what's happening in my inner world. By taking inventory, I deeply connect with my inner dialogue and conversations. I ask: *What are my dominant thoughts and feelings? What is my current state? What do I believe about myself today that gives rise to these thought-forms?*

A self-concept works best when it's present-tense, believable, and specific enough to guide action. Pick a new self-concept that feels slightly ahead of your current reality (a stretch, not a fantasy). Here are some general examples, but I encourage you to create ones that are more specific and try them all on:

- I am a person who has it all.
- I am a person who has spacious, joyful days and a steady and increasing income.
- I am a person who attracts aligned opportunities and says yes with clarity.
- I am a person who organizes my life so that creativity and peace coexist.

- I am a person who receives love, respect, and honest partnership and is worthy of being cherished.

Over time, I started imagining my self-concept from the perspective of a higher, more enlightened version of myself. Because ultimately, the only version of life we're ever "competing with" is a more expanded, evolved version of ourselves.

Most people's self-concepts often shift based on their internal experience and how they feel based on who they surround themselves with. (This relates to Rohn's five-person theory I mentioned in the previous chapter.) Have you ever changed your personality based on where you were or who you were with? For example, does your self-concept change when you are at work versus when you're at home? How does it change when you are with your romantic partner versus with your parents or close friends? Everyone "masks" to a certain degree around different people or while in different places, such as perhaps not cussing while at work, but it's important to recognize how your self-concept changes your behavior in different environments.

I suggesttaking an inventory of your identity and self-concept today and decide what new identity and self-concept you'd like to have instead. Neville Goddard speaks about living as if, or acting as if, from the state of consciousness and the self-concept of your future-self, from the perspective of the person you wish to be. What would you be feeling, thinking, and believing if you were living from a more evolved self-concept? In other words, instead of creating a plan in a linear manner (i.e., *I needto do X to get to* Y) for how you need to grow or work on yourself, imagine that you, in the present, are already looking out of your future self's eyeswith your future self's perspective of the world.

One example is when people talk about their weight or their health. You'll often hear some people say that they're on a diet, or that they need to take better care of themselves.But what if their identity was that of an athlete? If they were an athlete, they would likely not be on a diet, for example, but instead they would believe inherently that they were a healthy person and make choices to support that identity.

I have a good friend who was a former bodybuilder who competed in bodybuilding competitions over twenty years ago. And yet, even now, in her sixties, she is still one of the most fit people I know. She believes that she is still the fittest and strongest person in the room and takes action aligned with that identity. Her medical markers and physical condition read decades younger than her age. After hip surgery, her recovery was astonishingly fast; her doctors even marveled and urged her to write down what she did so it could help other patients. Her identity is one of an athlete, and her decisions, choices, beliefs, and more were going to be outputs of this self-concept.

What if your identity was "*New York Times*,best-selling author or CEO"? How would you show up? How would you act?

I think it's fun to try on different identities or think back to a time when you felt a certain identity. Whenever I have a low self-esteem day or moment of weakness in my life, I like to "pull from" moments in my life when I felt radiant, confident, and extraordinarily aligned with what was happening in my life and bring that identity and self-concept into the present moment.

I also like to look at others who have already accomplished what I desire and try to lean into that persona as an example for my own. I recommend that you also practice looking at others in your downtrodden moments to expand your own limits on your self-concept and to help you see outside of your own constructs of reality.

Ritual: Decide on Your New Self-Concept

Here is a ritual to try on new self-concepts. Putting new self-concepts into practice daily will help make them a reality.

1. Before bed, decide on *one* self-concept you will wear the next day.

2. Make it present tense, believable, and specific. Write one sentence, such as: "Today, I am an athlete" or "I am the person who has it all."

3. When you wake, embody that choice, and again, decide how you're going to walk through the world for the day.

Here are a couple of quick ways to remind yourself of your new self-concept throughout the day.

- **Posture reset**—Stand or sit tall for ten seconds, with a soft chest and slow breath. Say your line aloud, for example: "Today, I am an athlete."

- **Visual micro-rehearsal**—See your healthy decisions, see you eating healthy foods and getting rest, working out; feel the small win. Then, do one immediate, tiny action that aligns with your self-concept (pour yourself a nourishing green drink, for example).

Mindset Is Similar to Identity and Self-Concept Shifting

Whoever you think you are, you are.

When I was much younger, I used to get so frustrated whenever I'd hear someone say that I could change my life simply by changing my "mental attitude." So many people talk about mindset, and yet, I now understand there's truth in it — though it's more nuanced than just thinking differently. True transformation happens when we shift our self-concept — when we stop identifying with the background character who reacts to life, and instead become the main character who directs it.

Shifting your actions and behaviors is not only about mental attitude and your mindset; it's about self-concept and identity. But knowing this information is still not enough for you to change your self-concept—one must *practice*their improved self-concept daily in order to move into a different state of consciousness. Real change requires persistence — rehearsing your upgraded identity until it becomes second nature. This is the essenceof main character energy: choosing to live from the consciousness of authorship, where your thoughts, emotions, and actions align with the version of you who already holds the pen.

CHAPTER 5

Code #5: You Have Agency Over Your Feelings—Choose Certainty

Feeling is the prayer. Emotion is the magnet. Belief is the key.
—*Gregg Braden*

One of the most profound moments in *The Matrix* is when Neo stops looking for external proof and instead embodies certainty. Up until that point, he was questioning whether he is truly The One, waiting for confirmation from others, and doubting his own power.

But the moment he lets go of doubt, everything changes. The bullets that once threatened his life become irrelevant. They no longer affect him because he no longer *believes* they can. This is a powerful example of how certainty overrides external conditions.

When you fully assume a belief—without hesitation, without looking for validation—the world rearranges itself to reflect that inner conviction, that certainty. In this chapter, we examine just how significant your feelings can be and how having agency over your feelings and embodying the feelings you want to attract more of can drastically change your life.

Emotions vs. Feelings

It is my belief that our feeling states are the most important things to master in the ten energy codes of life. How we feel about ourselves often creates our actions, thoughts, and behaviors. We attract or repel people based on our inner conversations, and over time, we tune in to the frequencies of other people, places, and things that are in resonance with our own.

We are highly attuned to physical energy, like weather, gravity, heat, sound, and light, but many of us are disconnected from the subtle energy running through our own bodies. We treat our physical form as if it's a pet we barely pay attention to, rather than the vehicle through which we experience everything. We are hardly aware of the perception we have about ourselves.

Now, before we go into this rule in more detail, I want to share a quick distinction between emotional and feeling states. While emotions are temporary but automatic reactions to external stimuli, feelings are deep and sustained states that represent how we interpret our emotions. What I'm suggesting is that when we experience an emotion, we can decide how to translate—how to feel about—that emotion. To clarify the distinction between emotions and feelings, here is some more information:

- **Emotions are temporary reactions**
  - Emotions are automatic responses to external events or internal thoughts.
  - They arise from the unconscious mind, which constantly reacts to stimuli.
  - Emotions come and go quickly unless you continue to dwell on them.
  - Example: If someone insults you, you may feel anger or hurt instantly.

- **Feelings are deep, sustained states**
  - Feelings are prolonged states of consciousness that influence the subconscious mind.

○ Feelings are the stories we tell ourselves about the emotion we experienced.

○ Feelings are chosen states that we embody and maintain.

○ Example: If you repeatedly feel unworthy, you create a dominant feeling state of lack, which then manifests in your outer world.

I've said it before: No one and nothing can "make you" feel a certain way. Emotions and feelings are instead clues to help you navigate life. They are just data points. We can also take on other people's emotions and feelings through transference, and it's possible to sense a feeling that has come from outside of us. Knowing how to discern if a feeling has come from an outside stimulus versus inside of us is one of the most powerful awareness tools to master in order to accurately make sense of our feelings.

If you did take on an emotion or feeling that comes from outside of you, as one of my dear friends, lets call her Tina, would say: "Why would you choose to take this feeling state on? Why would you allow this person's feelings to come into your field and into your physical body? Why would you allow this person to make you feel differently about yourself?" If it did come from inside of you, then it's time to sit with the feelings and let them be, without any resistance or story. If the feelings are really intense, and you've tried sitting and feeling them for a while, I would suggest trying different breathwork exercises or working with a somatic therapist to help you move feelings out of your body.

Some modalities I've used in the past and can recommend are Tension and Trauma Release Exercises (TRE®), eye movement and desensitization and reprocessing (EMDR), breath work, Kundalini yoga, ecstatic dance, massage, and embodiment practices. Each of these methods is designed to move emotions through and out of the body.

Here are some explanations for these modalities:

- **TRE® (Tension and Trauma Release Exercises):** A method that activates the body's natural shaking mechanism to release stored stress and trauma.

- **EMDR (eye movement desensitization and reprocessing):** A therapy that helps process traumatic memories by using guided eye movements to rewire the brain's response to past events.

- **Breath work:** Conscious, deep breathing techniques that help release emotional blockages and regulate the nervous system.

- **Kundalini yoga:** A combination of movement, breath, and chanting that helps stimulate energy flow and release emotional tension.

- **Ecstatic dance:** Freeform movement practice where participants surrender to the rhythm and allow their bodies to move intuitively without choreography or judgment.

- **Massage:** Physical touch can help release tension stored in the muscles, which often hold unprocessed emotional energy.

- **Embodiment practices:** These focus on deep body awareness and presence, reconnecting with sensations rather than overanalyzing emotions. Examples include somatic experiencing and the Feldenkrais Method.

Many people try to process emotions only through thinking—but emotions live in the body. If they aren't fully felt and released, they can get stored in the nervous system, leading to chronic stress, physical pain, and emotional numbness. In *The Body Keeps the Score*, Dr. Bessel van der Kolk explores how emotions—especially those tied to trauma—are stored in the body, shaping our thoughts, behaviors, and overall well-being. Traumatic experiences become imprinted in the nervous system, leading to fight, flight, freeze, or fawn responses that often persist long after the danger has passed.

The Three *M*'s

Many people come to me stuck and have difficulty "shifting their feelings." They complain, saying, "I can't shift how I feel," and the answer isn't more thinking; it's more feeling. One of the fastest ways I know to change your inner state is simple, and I call it *the Three M's*: memory, music, movement.

Start with a memory: The first time you held a pet or child, that hush after an unexpectedly good yoga class, a sunset that made your chest open. Sit in that memory until the sensation moves through you. Don't analyze, just remember the feeling.

Turn on a song that matches that feeling. Music is instant recalibration: One chorus or tune can change your posture, widen your breath, and tune your nervous system back to an open heart and possibility. My friend Brandy Gillmore speaks about music's magic for shifting states—we explored this on my show *Gateways to Awakening*. I recommend building a go-to playlist you can pull up whenever you need to change your inner weather. We'll also talk more about which songs to choose later in the chapter.

And if the feeling still won't clear, get up and move. Shake, sway, stomp, dance, whatever your body asks. Animals shake off stress for a reason. Just getting up and shaking alone for a few minutes a day could have a major impact on your physiology.

Personally, when I incorporated the Three *M*'s and breath work into my life, I noticed a radical shift in my body. I began to feel more safe and energized and less stressed overall, and it became easier to process new feelings. This was the point when I truly gained agency over my feelings and my life started to change in quantum leaps before my eyes.

You Can Decide Your Feelings

You decide how you're going to feel and what you will "take on." So decide today that you will not allow external feeling states or transference into your field. Even with this decision, it's possible that your boundaries may not be completely effective, so stay on guard against any feelings that are not your own that begin to creep in.

As for feeling states that start inside of us, I believe these are just clues given to us by our soul about the past. We may have inherited these feeling states, or we may have formed these feeling states based on our identity or past behavior. But we are not meant to *dwell* in these low or bad feeling states. We are meant to use them as data points to decide what to do about a person or situation.

We all have a default feeling state, which can oscillate anywhere from fear to desire to courage to love and bliss. Many of us yo-yo between feeling states and have a difficult time choosing which feeling state to embody. We are often reacting to our existing cocktail of emotions and rarely take a step back and design our day based on how we *want* to feel. This concept is what led Neville Goddard to develop the Law of Assumption, which states that your assumptions—what you believe and assume to be true—shape your reality.

Remember my suggestion at the end of the last chapter to wake up each day and decide on your new self-concept by the end of the day? One of my friends taught me that exercise, but it can go even further. Upon waking up, decide how you're going to feel by the end of the day. I started to do this when I lived in Los Angeles: I'd wake up in the morning and decide that by the end of the day, I'm going to feel cherished and loved. And by the end of the day, I would! The external world would meet my inner state and reflect that back to me. This is also an amazing exercise that is adaptable in many ways, and I encourage you to experiment with it.

Like in the exercise above, living your present moment as if from the end goal is the most direct way to shift timelines. When we embody the feeling of already having what we desire, our consciousness naturally aligns with that reality, and begins to reflect it back.

Why Certainty?

Certainty is one of the most powerful feeling states to master. I learned this from the Kabbalists, specifically from Michael Berg and David Ghiyam. The feeling of certainty is about having absolute faith in a higher power and order that is orchestrating a greater plan. There have been so many times I've looked back on my life and marveled because things worked out so much better than I could have imagined. And yet, in the moment, I wasn't always so sure that would be the case because there would be things that happened that seemed to signal the opposite. I remember feeling so frustrated when things wouldn't go my way, and looking back now, I feel like I blocked the natural flow of energy at times and made things harder than they needed to be.

Beyond certainty, I believe that faith in the unknown and that things will work out is a superpower. Oftentimes, we get what we want in life, but it's usually at the expense of our well-being, our energy, our life force. I believe that when we lean into faith, trust, and certainty, synchronicities appear, showing that we are in the right place at the right time. I've certainly seen this play out in my life. The moment I lean back, let go, and surrender to a greater intelligence, I see so much magic unfold in the most unexpected ways. I often become the magnet that attracts things that are looking for me, rather than exerting force to get them. The way of ease, flow, and more faith is a much easier way to walk through life rather than pure willpower. It signals to the outer world that we have full faith in things working out for our highest good and that we do not need to understand or see the full story in order to do so.

I believe we can direct our feeling states throughout the day. Going back to the ritual in the previous chapter on deciding on your new self-concept to act out the next day, I often set an intention of a feeling state for each major activity of the day. You can even start with a simple intention for the morning, noon, and evening. While this can be done at any point of the day as well, it is extra helpful to determine which feeling states will be best for the different activities that are planned for the day.

For instance, if I have an important meeting that day and later I'm having dinner with my friends, I'll decide that I will feel powerful during my meeting and I will feel happy and cherished when meeting up with friends. This is especially helpful when I'm not necessarily feeling these things when I wake up. And before I go into the meeting and before dinner, I will reiterate these feeling states to myself as a reminder of my intentions.

Some people might think this is wacky, but what could be more valuable than deciding how you're going to feel for the day rather than leaving it up to chance and the external world? If you don't set an intention for the day, you'll likely get pulled off your own movie stage and become a supporting character in someone else's. This is one of the most common ways that we lose our power, and lose our main character status. Why would we want to be a victim to our historical feeling states or the feeling states of those around us? Many of us often ride the emotions and feelings of others and usually cannot even discern where our feelings start and where another person's ends.

Method Acting: When Feelings Become Too Real

One method that we can look to for inspiration is method acting, a popular acting technique that world-class Hollywood actors utilize to get into character. Method acting evolved from the actor-training system of Konstantin Stanislavski in the early twentieth century and was reshaped in the United States by teachers such as Lee Strasberg, Stella Adler, and Sanford Meisner.

At its core, the method asks the performer to "live truthfully under imaginary circumstances": to use imagination, sense-memory, and affective rehearsal so the body and nervous system respond as if the role were real. By repeatedly embodying a character's posture, breath, sensations, and emotional tone, the actor conditions habitual responses—voice, gesture, attention—so the performance becomes an authentic, automatic expression of that assumed identity. Everyone from Robert De Niro, Jack Nicholson, Daniel Day-Lewis, Adrien Brody, Christian Bale, Joaquin Phoenix, and Sean Penn have used this method in their movies. Method acting trains the nervous system to accept a new identity, which is exactly what Neville Goddard teaches about manifestation.

However, this can also work against you when you dwell in negative or difficult emotions and feeling states. There is a dark side to assuming a negative state. Actors like Heath Ledger, Philip Seymour Hoffman, River Phoenix, and even Daniel Day-Lewis have been known to go to extreme lengths to embody their characters. Some fell into addiction, depression, or suffered from psychological distress because they internalized their roles too deeply.

For example, Heath Ledger, while acting as the Joker in *The Dark Knight*, kept a journal filled with disturbing imagery and isolated himself, which some believe contributed to his mental decline. Adrien Brody, another method actor who played the protagonist in *The Pianist*, gave up his apartment, sold his belongings, and starved himself for the role. It took him over a year to feel "normal" again. By making the role *feel* real, the body and mind respond as if it *is* real. The danger is that if an actor assumes a dark or painful state and their subconscious accepts it as truth, I believe that they may carry that energy into their personal life.

You see, the mind doesn't necessarily distinguish between reality and assumption. As Neville Goddard teaches, when you assume a feeling state consistently, it imprints on the subconscious mind and begins to shape external reality.

Because of this, I believe there is danger in overexposing ourselves to images or experiences that might stimulate a feeling state that we personally don't want to experience. An example of this is watching horror or violent movies, or playing video games where your role is to be a war leader. But you can also change your feeling states by experiencing art and media that emits frequencies of positivity and a sense of calm.

Choosing Positive Feeling States

As mentioned earlier, I also believe musical lyrics and sonic textures act like soft programmers on our feeling states. On *Gateways to Awakening,* in the episode "Conscious Music Consumption and Why Your Voice Matters," I spoke with Madame Gandhi, who argued that music is not neutral: The songs we choose to listen to shape what we feel, what we can imagine, and what we tolerate in the world. Her TED Talk is a reminder that music carries messages, frames experiences, and that conscious listening matters. Many lyrics and musical themes, when heard repeatedly and in everyday contexts, influence mood, norms, and even prosocial or risky behaviors over time. I always urge people to be very careful about what type of music lyrics they listen to, as over time, they tend to impact our inner state.

Madame Gandhi urges listeners to become intentional about what they play and amplify because repeated exposure to particular themes (misogyny, violence, objectification, etc.) helps normalize them, whereas conscious curation can model healthier values and emotional tonality. She also frames music-listening as an ethical practice: both listeners and creators carry responsibility. Listeners can "audit" their soundtracks (on commutes, workout playlists, background music) and choosetracks that cultivate empathy, clarity, and the world they want to live in. Creators can be deliberate about the stories and moods they seed into culture.

Now, I assume that whoever is reading this wants to immerse themselves in positive feeling states or at least desire a sense of agency over consciously creating their feeling states rather than unconsciously immersing themselves in a feeling that is less desirable. The good news is that you can choose what sort of media and experiences you immerse yourself in. You can choose to experience things that uplift you. For example, if you attend a talk by an inspirational or motivational leader, or watch a romantic film that inspires you to open yourself up to a relationship, you're also consciously choosing a reality that will provide more calm, love, creativity, and peace.

So, which feeling state will you choose to embody? They can be more than a simple "empathetic" or "happy." Some of my favorite feeling states include:

- Something magical just happened.
- My life is one big celebration.
- I am standing at the edge of something extraordinary.
- I belong everywhere I go.

- I have certainty in the greater plan for my life.

- My presence shifts the energy in every room I enter.

- My life is a never-ending dream life where I get to experience joy, passion, and creativity.

Are Your Conversations Mutually Beneficial?

Another thing to consider when mindfully choosing what feelings to embrace and which are not in your best interest is who you spend your time with and what kinds of feeling states they inspire. It took some time and practice, but I have found that being aware of how my "friends" communicate with me can clue me in on if they are aligned with me in a mutually beneficial way.

Many people are wildly underdeveloped in the art of both listening and communication, which is often why there is so much misunderstanding and defensiveness in relationships. I used to be one of these people. I did not have the skill set to have difficult conversations, and with the help of many mentors, teachers, and guides, I was able to work on my ability to effectively communicate.

What I learned is that there are four ways to communicate and listen:

1. The first way we can communicate is where one person is sharing and the other person is in the space of witness. They are not responding but simply there to hold space and listen.

2. The second way to communicate is where one person is sharing and the other person reflects *only* what they're saying back to them to ensure the first person knows they're being seen and understood.

3. The third way to communicate is where one person is sharing and the other person shares their personal related experiences, feedback, perspective, and suggestions.

4. The fourth way to communicate is where one person is sharing and the other person shares their perspective as if they were a coach, giving very specific advice and actionable next steps.

Here is a crucial practical rule I use: Unless someone asks for coaching, don't give it. It's tempting to jump into problem-solving or to offer feedback, but doing so without permission often imposes your movie on someone else's. This is one of the greatest lessons I had to learn on my journey, especially when, in some cases, I would get intuitive messages— a clear image, word, sensation, or knowing that seems to appear out of nowhere as someone is speaking. Over time, I realized that not every message I received was meant to be shared. Some insights arrive simply to help us hold space with deeper understanding. Respecting another person's sovereignty is a sacred act of energetic integrity — and one of the clearest signs of true intuitive maturity.

Instead, slow down and ask one simple question when in conversation: "Are you looking for feedback, reflection, or just for me to listen?" That single clarification honors the other person's process, protects your field, and keeps the exchange constructive. When you ask first, you preserve the integrity of both your energy and the relationship, and you create the conditions for real help instead of unconscious draining.

Have you ever left a conversation with a friend or colleague feeling drained or exhausted? Now, look, I know that relationships should be spaces where people feel comfortable sharing what's on their mind and where people are able to find some kind of refuge and solace. But every time we interact with someone, we are exchanging energy, and we have to be able to discern if the person we're speaking with is trying to hold us back from evolving and growing into a greater version of ourselves, even if they are doing it unconsciously. It's important to discern if people truly want to have a generative conversation that is in service to something greater, or if there is a "dumping" energy, in which one person unloads their problems onto another without asking for explicit permission and consent. I believe it is important to gather enough self-awareness in ourselves to understand if we're ever doing that to another person as well.

I think the reason why most people don't grow is because of their limited and comfortable social network. In other words, the reason why most people don't change is because of other people.

I also encourage you to always see the absolute best in others and see them living their best and greatest life. We can only expand and grow at the boundaries of our self-concept, and we can help others expand theirs by seeing greater versions of them. In other words, we expand at the "ceiling" of who we think we are. To help someone grow, we can show them a believable next version of themselves and invite them to take one small step toward it.

Growth happens at the *edges*, where your current belief about yourself meets something you haven't yet accepted as true. When you push gently on those edges, you open new habits, skills, and possibilities; when you push too hard, you trigger defensive resistance. We need people in our lives who can expand our own self-concept and sense of self. And the reverse is true: Oftentimes, people don't shift because the people around them want them to stay the same, or even worse, compete with them.

Complaining & Pricey Conversations

In my Inner Knowing School, I often create a Forty-Day No Complaining Challenge with many of my clients, which I like to participate in as well. This is a powerful challenge because it can dramatically shift your feeling state in a relatively short period of time. The reason why I select forty days is that the forty-day period is often cited as a minimum duration for breaking negative habits and cultivating positive ones in my yoga tradition. I've tested this myself and found it to be true.

The idea is to not create any negative commentary about others or situations (external), nor about yourself (internal). You can either be neutral or look for what you appreciate in a person or situation. If you want to commit to the No Complaining Challenge, it's helpful to gather forward momentum by keeping yourself accountable and making it easy to remember. Write it on a piece of paper, and put it on your fridge or on the mirror. You could even create a Complaining Jar, where, like a Swear Jar, you put loose change in the jar each time you complain. Making this commitment is a great step toward a start to a new behavioral pattern. Once we recalibrate our energy and feeling state to one of appreciation and gratitude, we'll resonate with the experiences and situations we want instead. We'll resonate with people who are focusing on being the best versions of themselves because that is the frequency we are also putting out into the world.

Ritual: Mini No Complaining Challenge

Why don't you give it a try? For the next seven days, commit to a No Complaining Challenge of your own. That means no complaining in your inner world and outer world. No complaining with your friends and family, and no gossip. The idea here is to look for what's right and what's working instead, and not give any energy and attention to what's not working.

People who often look for what's wrong in people and situations or criticize profusely will often experience a reality in which people will disappoint them, or they will invite criticism from others. The less you criticize yourself or others, you release yourself from immersing in any negative feeling states for extended periods of time. You release yourself from going into a neural network from the past that didn't serve you.

I tried this first in 2014 when I lived in NYC, and my life dramatically changed. I remember how serene my life felt and how so many new possibilities opened up for me. A new career path emerged seemingly out of nowhere, and I rode a wave into a life that was completely different from the one I built in my twenties. Everything I desired seemingly came to me, and every single friend felt incredibly safe around me because they knew that not only would I not participate in gossip with others, and I would no longer be in spaces where anyone did. My life had become easy and harmonious. I remember physically getting up and walking away from conversations where people would slide into what I now call "pricey conversations."

Like I said earlier, we're either investing our energy or spending it. All day, every day.

Pricey conversations are the ones that cost you. They pull the group's frequency downward—through complaining, gossip, judgment, or subtle ridicule of someone not present. There's no desire for resolution, no curiosity, no healing; they're just venting, projecting, and low-grade tearing others down. And while these conversations may seem harmless in the moment, they're energetically expensive. They drain your vitality, lower your vibration, and reinforce disconnection instead of expansion.

It's not just one conversation—it's the energetic domino effect that follows, the emotional residue, the neural grooves that deepen and the old stories that are reactivated. Pricey conversations pull you into patterns that don't serve your highest self. Remember: Your energy is your life force. That's your power in this lifetime.

I've always wondered: Why do people gather just to drain each other? Why not gather to amplify? To elevate? To speak life into one another? To walk away more alive than when you arrived?

That's the room I want to be in.

Now, that's usually the only room I'm interested in joining these days.

But like all spiritual paths, mine hasn't been linear. I've lost my way more than once—sometimes because of just one or two frustrated people whose energy I allowed to distort my own.

Still, I always return to this lesson: When I protect my peace, hold my frequency, and stay rooted in joy and alignment, life responds with so much magic.

So join me on a Seven-Day No Complaining challenge to start and work your way up to the forty-day challenge. You can set up a ritual for yourself to have a daily check-in prompt: *Where, when, and with whom did I catch myself complaining today?*

Here is a mantra you can use whenever you complain: *I choose to redirect my energy to what I want instead. I create the script of my life. I don't react.*

Having agency over your feelings and feeling states means creating and projecting a sense of certainty in yourself and how you want to live your life, and when you choose this certainty, the world will automatically shift to meet your conviction. This leads us to our next code: how our external world mirrors our inner world.

CHAPTER 6

Code #6: Your Outer Reality Is a Mirror of Your Inner World

Change your conception of yourself and you will automatically change the world in which you live. Do not try to change people; they are only messengers telling you who you are. Revalue yourself and they will confirm the change.
—Neville Goddard

When the Oracle tells Neo that he's not The One, she plants a seed of doubt. Yet, this statement becomes a self-fulfilling prophecy—Neo remains uncertain about his identity until he fully believes in his own power.

The moment he embraces the truth that he *is* The One, reality shifts to confirm it. Neo's journey shows that reality does not validate our potential until we first accept it as true within ourselves.

This perfectly illustrates the Mirror Principle—the idea that the external world reflects our internal beliefs—which is the basis for the sixth energy mastery code. This chapter focuses on the Mirror Principle, which is also known as karma, cause and effect, and the Law of Resonance, and you'll see me refer to it by these other names in this book, but there's also often a time delay between what energy you put out into the world and how that energy comes back to you. As I'll explain, the Universe will come to collect on how you use your energy, so instead of reacting to it in a way that will only promote more negativity in your life, remember that you can break the cycle by focusing on what you *want* to create and attract in your life.

The Law of Resonance

Our feeling states, thoughts, beliefs, intentions, and memories emit an energetic frequency into the Universe, and that frequency carries a resonance that shapes our reality. Every emotion we experience generates a vibrational frequency, much like a note played on an instrument. The outward ripple represents the energy we project into the Universe, while the inward ripple reflects how the Universe "echoes" back a resonance that aligns with our original vibration. This is the Law of Resonance in action. For example, feelings of joy, gratitude, and self-love generate high-frequency vibrations, while fear, anger, and despair emit lower frequencies. We attract what we resonate, not what we want. Many of us continuously cycle through patterns about worthiness and what we think we deserve, and the world often mirrors it back to us.

Let me give you an explanation of the Law of Resonance from Dr. Ibrahim Karim, who is an architect and the founder of BioGeometry, which is a holistic science that focuses on the "energy of shape" to achieve harmony and balance of energy systems within an environment. He says: "The only way that [a physical shape] can [contain multidimensional subtle energy levels] is through resonance.... Think of instruments. For example, if you hit one string, every string with double or half its length will resonate with it. The Law of Resonance goes from zero to infinity." Isn't that fascinating?

And just like how musical notes resonate with each other, our frequency is constantly interacting with the world around us, creating a harmonic symphony that attracts experiences, people, and circumstances that match or complement our energetic state. We'll also often instinctively feel when our frequency is out of tune with a person, place, or situation—an internal discord that signals misalignment.

This law took me the absolute longest time to master, and it's still one that I have to work on deeply. My feelings used to be created based on my reactions to the outside world. I felt that things in the outside world were happening *to* me rather than reflecting *back* to me my inner dialogue, beliefs, thoughts, and frequency state. This happened over and over again. I felt like I had to control my outer world in order to feel a sense of inner peace in my inner world. But I was only chasing my own tail.

As we explored in the last chapter, while emotions are spontaneous reactions to external stimuli, feelings are the deeper, sustained states that emerge from our internal interpretations. Emotions may be fleeting, but the feeling states we cultivate determine our dominant frequency. When we shift our internal state—through awareness, intention, and practice—we shift the energetic signals we send out into the world. Our inner frequency becomes the magnet for our external reality. If we want to shift our lives, it begins by shifting our inner state. This isn't an intellectual exercise; it's a practice—a daily commitment to self-awareness and recalibration.

What I've noticed, both in my own life and in my work with others, is that many people struggle to manifest what they truly want because they're focused outward. They attempt to change external circumstances without first transforming their internal feeling state and inner resonance. True manifestation requires turning inward and asking, *What would I be feeling if I already had that which I desire? How would the new version of me—who already has what I want—think, feel, and act?*

Through my work with executives and my intuition school, I've observed a profound truth: Time doesn't matter. Transformation happens when belief, feelings, and practice intersect; the real change happens when you step into the version of yourself that already embodies your desires and maintains coherence between your thoughts, feelings, actions, and, ultimately, frequency.

You always receive that which you resonate with.

We must close the gap between where we are and where we want to be not by chasing the external but by becoming internally vibrationally aligned with the life and the feeling state that we seek.

The Mirror Doesn't Always Reflect in Real Time

An interesting thing I've noticed about the Mirror Principle is that it doesn't necessarily follow linear time. When a thought or energy form is thrown out into the world, it does not always return it in real time. There is a sort of invisible accounting ledger of energy. Whenever we are out of balance, that energy comes to collect with interest and perhaps over-indexes on what we "borrowed" or took out. I mentioned this concept of the Universe coming to collect debts in chapter 3 as well when discussing the hierarchies of importance we create, which distorts the energy around us.

The energetic ripples from the Mirror Principle take time to return, often coming back at an unexpected time or in a surprising form. For example, if you are judging someone in your life, or if you feel superior toward someone, then this mirror response might come to collect in another situation entirely or with the same person but in some other time and situation and, usually, when you least expect it.

I also believe that the mirror principle is similar to the Law of Karma. This law states that all actions have consequences; causes set in motion affects that return to the doer in time. When you act (you throw the stone, for example), you create energetic and practical effects that travel outward and ripple back. Over time, this loop becomes a stable feedback system; your thoughts, beliefs, and habits produce environments that reinforce those habits. Buddhist and Hindu teachings about karma also suggest that the world is not merely an arena of random cause; your inner life shapes what you encounter.

An Inner Knowing

I'll give you an example of the mirror principle at play in my own life. In this instance, the Universe came to collect pretty quickly and somewhat ironically.

One instance was in 2023 when I was on my way to Erewhon Market in Santa Monica to meet my beloved yoga teacher, who was an absolute beast in the world of business. It was my first time going to Erewhon Market, which is a bougie supermarket.

Having just moved from the Bay Area, I had very little patience for fancy supermarkets, and even less patience for supermarkets with valet parking. As we approached Erewhon, she called to tell me to valet my car.

Valet my car? I thought to myself. *At a supermarket?*

Yikes. I was firmly in resistance to that idea and started thinking about how expensive Santa Monica was. I found myself immersed in thoughts of scarcity and judgment. Determined to resist playing into the valet option, I found a parking meter nearby and parked at the meter instead.

I haughtily walked over to Erewhon Market to meet my friend. As we were sitting and eating lunch, I started seeing images in my mind's eye—pictures of me getting a parking ticket.

I turned to her and said, "I think I'm getting a ticket."

"Well, did you pay the meter?" she asked.

I nodded. "Yes, I did."

"Then relax," she said.

She didn't know that I am clairaudient and sometimes clairvoyant—and sure enough, when I got back to my car, I saw that I had a seventy-five dollar parking ticket.

There was a sign on the street that said "No Parking 2–4 p.m. Tuesdays," and, of course, it just happened to be a Tuesday.

The old version of me would have been frustrated and dropped into a lower frequency state. But instead, I laughed. I looked at the ticket and laughed at myself—really hard.

Instead of blaming the outside world (the ticket, the police, the mirror), I decided to investigate myself—my inner thoughts, my scarcity mindset, my judgment. I realized that I received the ticket because I had been in a space of extreme judgment, and the world mirror simply said, "Okay, here you go."

The world mirror is always agreeing with what we believe, think, and feel. If we feel the world is scarce, we will find evidence of this scarcity in our external reality— our world mirror. The ripples of energy you send out interact with the "obstacles" and "edges" of the world— other people, events, and environments. This interaction can transform your energy in quantum leaps. A kind act might inspire a chain reaction of goodwill, and a deceitful act may bring about a betrayal. This is why we have to be *very* careful about our thoughts and our beliefs about people and situations. You certainly do not want to project anger, frustration, and judgement into the mirror because you will find yourself on the receiving end of these emotions and then you'll have the consequences that will "confirm" these feeling states.

To give you another example, consider the Evil Queen in *Snow White and the Seven Dwarfs.* The Evil Queen continuously asks her mirror if she is the most beautiful woman in the world. If someone was truly secure in themselves and their own value and inner beauty, they would not need to constantly ask for validation and reassurance from their outer world. Her constant inquiry symbolizes vanity, jealousy, and the destructive nature of ego-driven validation. And eventually, her inner world of hatred and malice turned against her.

Today, social media is the new "mirror on the wall." People post images of themselves, their lives, their achievements—not always for self-expression but for validation. They wait for likes, comments, and reactions, seeking external proof of their worth. It's important to remember this aspect of the "mirror" in today's world where we are nearly all addicted to our phones.

When you look into the mirror for validation or some approval, it will mirror back to you just that—the lack of your own self-approval. Instead of looking directly into the mirror, have faith and trust in your own inner world and inner conversations. The mirror is just a reflection, and it should never be the driver of your life.

I've also been reflecting on how so many of us hand our power, our attention, our life force again and again to everything outside ourselves, always hoping the next person, the next post, the next compliment will fill the empty places inside of us. Like a restless tide, we chase validation. It lifts us, then leaves us wanting more, and we're already scanning the horizon for the next person to give us their approval. Imagine, instead, walking through the world without hunger for anyone's approval.

The Kabbalists and Hermeticists teach the concept "as above, so below"; the micro and the macro correspond because the same pattern repeats at every scale. Some examples are neurons compared to galaxy filaments, fingerprints and river deltas, DNA helices and spiral galaxies. Those comparisons are suggestive and help us see the same organizing principles at play. The golden ratio and the Fibonacci sequence are another set to include here. They appear in sunflower heads, pinecones, seashells, and in proportions that artists and architects have used for centuries. Fractals which are self-similar patterns that repeat at different scales, showing up in river systems and branching trees, in the bronchial network of the lungs, and in the neural web of the brain. A river's branching maps almost perfectly onto blood vessels and root systems.

This is what the *mirror world* refers to—not just in form, but in consciousness. The outer world mirrors the inner one. What you hold in thought, feeling, and belief reflects outward into the physical realm. Knowing the geometry of life is not enough; you must live in harmony with it. When your inner state vibrates in coherence with the reality you desire, the outer world adjusts to match that frequency.

I've also found that simply knowing this information is not enough; one needs to *practice* honing their thoughts, feelings, and emotions to be in alignment with the external reality they want to resonate with. Neville Goddard called this "deferred occupancy," which is the habit of *knowing* or *deciding* inwardly that you will be some future self but postponing actually *inhabiting* that state in the present moment. This is an "unlearning" exercise, as so much of our existing reality is about stimuli and our response. Something happens in our external world, and just like if we're playing a game of whac-a-mole, we respond immediately on instinct, so our inner world is almost entirely dictated by our outer world. The world is your mirror, waiting for you to remember that you are both the observer and the architect of what you see.

Most people try to "control" the mirror by attempting to fix it, but the mirror is just a reflection. It'd be like trying to fix your hair by touching the mirror rather than fixing your own hair—it's impossible. We cannot change or fix the mirror, as more of the same just comes back to us in different ways; we can only fix the self. The outer world is a set of data points pointing out our inner state. So pay attention to all the details of your external reality. If your external reality is not one that you're happy about, it's time to reflect on your inner world instead of looking at the mirror. Sit with your inner state and identify what may be working against you and what is working in your favor. When you shift your beliefs, thoughts, and behaviors, your outside world will begin to change.

Another way to interact with the mirror is to observe it without emotion. Try looking at your life as if you were the director who hired all these actors and actresses to act in your life's movie. Imagine the actors are playing roles in your life for you to learn about yourself. Then, turn on the lights and pause the movie. Take a look at your life's stage and the players in it. You are in charge of this movie, so what would you want to happen next?

Now that you understand the Mirror Principle, remember: reality reflects your internal world with perfect neutrality. It doesn't judge or correct—it simply mirrors your dominant state of being. If you believe the world is hard, it becomes hard. If you believe you are supported, evidence of that support begins to appear.

So take inventory of what is showing up around you. Notice what themes, emotions, or conversations keep repeating. What are these reflections trying to tell you about your inner dialogue? Are you being critical, impatient, or unkind—to others or to yourself? Do you secretly believe life is working against you? Instead of reacting to the outside world, what is it that you want to send to the mirror today?

Ritual: Smile at the reflection

Today, decide on your new self-concept at the start of each day, when you wake up. Who are you? What's the new identity that you are choosing today? What are the new thoughts, beliefs and actions that this new identity would take? When the world mirrors something old like fear, resistance, self-doubt—see it not as failure, but as feedback. Smile at the reflection, laugh to yourself, hold your new frequency steady, and let reality recalibrate.

Remember to Have Conviction

I've also noticed that many people have major subconscious, unconscious, and conscious blocks preventing them from moving forward with this new identity. Doubts and blocks are normal though. Even the great teachers have doubted. Abdullah, the mysterious figure who was believed to be Neville Goddard's mentor, often spoke about Neville having "quibbles" when he started to teach him the law of assumption and the manifestation. "Oh," he'd say whenever Neville came to him with doubts, "you couldn't do it…it would poison you, because you have quibbles," "Quibbles" are small intellectual objections, caveats, or "yes, but" thoughts that interrupt the felt assumption of a desired state. These quibbles are the mental reservations that prevent full emotional occupancy of an imaginal act and feeling state. For example, you imagine or decide one thing, then immediately qualify or doubt it, and waver, which neutralizes the creative feeling state

This being said, we must remember code #6: You have agency over your feelings, so choose certainty. The mirror of life rewards certainty in oneself and one's conviction of self-concept. According to Abdullah, there are "no half measures in faith." One must fully accept the reality of one's desire as already done in imagination, without mentally debating its possibility.

He also said to let go of the "how." The moment you start questioning *how* something will happen, you are moving out of faith and into doubt. In other words, one must enter the desired state in imagination and *view the world from it* and not contest how the means will appear. You must have absolute inner conviction, and you must embody the feeling of already having what you desire with zero resistance.

If one can hold the state of faith in their new identity and persist in that, the outer world will have no choice but to mirror that back. Your inner conversations, feeling states, and the frequencies that you project ultimately shape your outer world. So shift your focus inward. Change your beliefs, emotions, and assumptions—and then trust that the world will reflect back a new, magical reality that reflects what your heart truly wants. With that in mind—and heart—we turn to the next code.

CHAPTER 7

Code #7: Listen to Your Heart for Signs of Alignment

I suggest that you try to create only from within the sacred space of the heart, for the heart knows only unity and will create the intention as it is conceived without its dark side.
—Drunvalo Melchizedek

I n the final battle, Neo moves beyond Intellect—he stops merely analyzing the Matrix and begins feeling the reality of his power. The moment his heart and mind align, he transcends the system and bends reality to his will.

Logic alone is not enough—true transformation happens when deep knowing and alignment take precedence over mere intellect. In this chapter we'll go over energy mastery code #7, which focuses on listening to your heart and finding or embracing what makes your heart feel full. We'll also examine some of the most powerful research on the heart that I've come across or have heard about in my discussions with many teachers across modalities. But while the heart brings much wisdom to situations, life choices, and what you seek to create or bring to the world, it's the combination of the heart *and* the mind that brings true balance and harmony to your life.

When Your Soul Stirs

We can usually tell when something we read or watch was created from the heart or from the mind. The difference is quite stark and nuanced.

The questions to ask yourself to determine this are: Did you feel inspired and moved or simply entertained? Did your soul stir after the experience? If it stirred something deeper within you and brought you closer to your heart, then it was likely created from a place of true authenticity and feeling.

While living in New York City, I wrote my first screenplay. *A Star in the Desert* is a story about a boy who retreats into an imagined underworld during the first Gulf War. At the time, I didn't know it would ever become a film, let alone an award-winning one. I was working a corporate job, and though I'd taken a few evening film classes at The New School, I had no real intention of breaking into the film world. So many people write scripts, and many even move to Los Angeles with a dream to produce a show or story they wrote.

When I wrote it, I only thought of this short script as a dream—a dream so captivating and heart-wrenching that I had to write it down. Looking back, I now understand that the reason why my first short film did so well was because it was written from my heart. The creative life force that birthed that script came from a place of divine inspiration beyond the veil. It was a place that came from the deep recesses of my heart, my Higher Self.

While sitting to write *A Star in the Desert*, I cried the entire time. I felt every painstaking emotion my main character, a young boy on the eve of a war, would experience. It was almost like the story was *given* to me. I saw the scenes creep into my consciousness one by one over a period of six months. And I knew it was special because anytime anyone read it, they would also respond with a powerful, moving reaction.

With the help of an amazing crew, *A Star in the Desert* came to life on screen. Looking back, I see the power of a story crafted from the heart, free from recycled narratives and touched by something beyond me. This experience taught me that when we listen deeply, the creative process becomes a bridge to something greater, something that resonates on a soul level.

Let Your Heart Guide You

We all know when we're speaking from a place of heart and mind coherence—when the heart and mind are in agreement and harmony as to the decisions we're making in life.

Many of us assign the title "CEO" to our mind and "COO" to our hearts, when it should be the reverse. The heart should be the CEO of our life, and the mind should be the COO. The heart is the guide, and the mind checks in to see if it can accomplish what the heart wants. Usually, when that's the case, life moves smoothly without any major roadblocks.

Whenever I am in touch with my heart or in "creation" mode, I am usually *not* using pure logic to move my ideas forward. Instead, I am sailing on the wind of an energy that brings wisdom from another space and time. Whenever I create from the heart, it has a perennial and timeless quality to it. Instead of piecing together a project rationally, the project is built through a primordial wisdom and a higher intelligence than what I would have access to in a linear, mind-led framework.

Have you ever had a desire, only to finally receive it and realize how much baggage came along with it? A wisdom teacher recently told me that when a desire comes from the mind, it comes from the ego, and it will always have a duality and a shadow side, and that duality will always play out in reality. For example, if a person desires to be a well-known speaker, then even when they attain that desire, that might play out in serious financial and emotional consequences in their personal or professional lives down the line.

If a desire, however, comes from the heart, then when that desire manifests, it will represent a unity consciousness, and the shadow side will not play out.

When I tell people about this distinction, a lot of people ask, "What does it mean to make a decision from your heart?" A heart-led decision is one that feels inspired and aligned. In other words, you don't have to convince yourself of the decision. You know that whatever you chose was meant for you and intended for you, rather than for someone else.

Most people tend to create based on inspiration from their social circles instead of the whisperings of their own heart. I used to do the same thing, making a lot of decisions based on social conditioning and what was considered "acceptable" to my peers. These choices would often lead me down roads that were filled with people, places, and things that depleted my energy and took me far off my path. Years later, I would look back and wonder, *What the heck happened? How did I end up here?*

I'll give you an overview of my journey learning to listen to my heart. In my twenties I made the majority of my decisions from my mind. I also bought into the competitive ego nature of my social circle in NYC, where most people's favorite pastimes were to brag about what home they lived in and the restaurants they went to, and talk excessively about their lifestyle.

Truthfully, I didn't know what I really wanted. I had no connection with the whisperings of my heart. I was distracted and mostly entertained while I lived in NYC but certainly not inspired. I didn't feel like I was in harmony.

When I look back on those years, I am often shocked at how meaningless a lot of it was. I acquired a lot of outward success, and yet inside both emotionally and physically, I was completely out of balance and out of coherence.

By the time I hit my thirties, I had to make a major course correction. I started living from my heart, and for me, that meant leaving the corporate world and creating space. Success to me now is having a sense of inner peace and a regulated nervous system.

These days, I don't let more than an hour go by without noticing if I've wandered off the path of my heart. I know when I'm off path because my external world will start to give me clues. This is just like what we discussed in previous chapters: When things are out of balance in your inner world, your outer world will start to show that. It's really that simple.

And I've certainly made my fair share of mistakes and not followed my heart. Many years ago, for example, I entered a serious romantic partnership with someone who seemed like a good guy and would be a good father, and yet after our first few dates, I wrote in my journal that I felt something wasn't right.

My heart did not feel aligned. And yet, I was mentally saying yes because it appeared that he checked a lot of boxes in my relationship checklist.

This is a perfect example of the mind justifying something that did not give me a full body *yes.*At best, it felt neutral with flickers of happiness every now and then. And whenever we need to justify a decision or a situation, especially to ourselves, we've definitely veered off the path of the heart. We don't need to justify anything in our lives, be it prestige or external validation, to convince ourselves of any decisions we make, whether it's in romantic partnership or in business.

Especially since then, it's been important for me to be aware of when my desires come from an authentic and inspired place or if it comes from a place of social conditioning. If something feels expansive and light, that usually means you're headed in the right direction. If something feels constrained and dark, or even uninteresting, then it means that you're likely not aligned with your heart.

Let your heart guide you in the major decisions in your life, and you will live a life that is balanced and expansive.

Heart Research

Based on my podcast interviews and my own research, there are so many case studies and research from various modalities and teachers that speak about the heart. I'll spend this section going over some of the most powerful discussions and definitions that I've read and heard about.

I had the privilege of interviewing the late Brenda Dunn, the former head of research at the Princeton Engineering Anomalies Research Lab, on my podcast before she passed. She was an amazing woman who studied intuition for over thirty years and found that "intuition is accessing information from the heart rather than the head." She says that "when we allow the inner self to communicate with us, we get valuable information." I thought it was especially interesting that intuition should be more associated with the heart than the mind, as people often think of intuition as being almost like a mind-reading power.

The HeartMath Institute, a research and educational organization on the science of heart-brain connection, explains that "Heart Coherence," a term specific to the HeartMath Institute, "is a state of cooperative alignment between the heart, mind, and emotions." In this state, our heart rhythm becomes more ordered and harmonious. Achieving Heart Coherence is particularly important when making decisions because it helps us access a more intuitive perspective.

Carlos Castaneda, an anthropologist and writer who is one of the fathers of Toltec wisdom, speaks of a complex concept known as the "assemblage point," which he was able to access through various exercises meant to shift awareness. Located just slightly off center in the chest, this is a "valve of consciousness" according to Castaneda, the place through which reality is interpreted and experienced.

In Christian and esoteric traditions, the cross is symbolic of the junction between the vertical (divine/spiritual) and the horizontal (earthly/material) realms, or between human experience and divine consciousness. From a mystical perspective, if the cross is superimposed on the human body, the intersection is often placed at the heart center, where spirit (the vertical axis) meets physical form (the horizontal axis). This resonates with the concept of the heart assemblage point, as both represent the place where perception and reality are shaped.

Another well-known teacher, Drunvalo Melchizedek, a spiritual teacher and author of many books including *Flower of Life, Volumes 1–3*, emphasizes the connection between the heart and sacred geometry in his teachings. He introduces the concept of a "sacred space within the heart," a place of pure consciousness and unity with creation. Accessing this space allows individuals to experience a deeper connection to the Universe and their true selves.

While I have not interviewed Drunvalo, I did interview Viola Rose, one of a hundred teachers on the planet allowed to teach his work, on my podcast. When speaking with Viola Rose, I learned that the heart space is a place where ideas and inspiration are revealed.

Drunvalo teaches that the heart space is beyond the mind and intellect, offering a portal to the divine and our true essence. While the mind analyzes and creates dualities, the heart offers direct knowing. Rose adds that "The mind is a perfect tool for navigating this world of duality, but it was never meant to run the show. The heart holds the key to unity and peace." Drunvalo goes on to explain that the heart's energy field, the *torus*, is a vital connection to the infinite and reflects the structure of the Universe. In his book *Living in the Heart*, he says, "I am convinced that the toroidal electromagnetic field passes exactly through and is generated from the sacred space of the heart." Both Renée Garcia and Vadim Zeland speak extensively about heart and mind coordination. According to Zeland, true power and effortless movement through reality come when the heart (soul) and mind (intellect) are in harmony. But most people experience internal conflict— where the mind wants one thing, but the heart feels differently—which creates resistance and disharmony. In fact, Zeland says that "the mind is constantly generating thoughts, and the voice of the heart is literally drowned out by the 'thought-churn,' making it difficult to access intuitive knowledge." Renée Garcia, thought leader, founder of the International Transurfing Institute, and author of *Quantum Capitalist*, similarly, believes that when individuals harmonize their heart's desires with their mind's intentions, they can effectively navigate the quantum field to manifest their desired reality.

Taking a more biological perspective, Bruce Cryer, another guest on my podcast and a co-founder of the Heart-Math Institute, explains that the heart is not just a pump; it is an intelligent system with its own neural network. He says that the heart and brain are in constant communication, with the heart sending four times more information to the brain than the brain sends to the heart.

When the heart, for example, is in a chaotic heart rhythm, caused by stress or anxiety, distorted signals are sent to the brain, impairing cognitive function and decision making. In contrast, a coherent heart rhythm supports clarity, focus, and emotional resilience.

Some techniques to achieve heart coherence, Cryer explained, include focusing on feelings of love, gratitude, or appreciation for as little as fifteen seconds at a time, which can transform chaotic heart patterns into a smooth sine, wave-like rhythm. Heart and Mind coherence is highly trainable, accessible to people of all ages, and creates an internal environment conducive to better decision making, creativity, and health.

Another coherence technique is to focus your attention on your breath. Begin by focusing on the area of your heart. Breathe slowly and deeply, imagining the oxygen flowing in and out through your heart, approximately five seconds per inhale and exhale. Consciously cultivate a positive emotion, such as gratitude or appreciation, for a person, experience, or moment.

Cryer shared a true story from Paul Pearsall's book *The Heart's Code* that seemed unbelievable and, yet, may suggest that the heart does carry memory. An eight-year-old girl received a heart transplant from a ten-year-old girl who had been tragically murdered. After the surgery, the heart recipient began experiencing vivid and recurring nightmares of being attacked. The dreams were so specific that they included detailed descriptions of the assailant, the murder weapon, and the crime's location. The intensity and clarity of these dreams were unlike anything the child had experienced before.

Intrigued by the consistency of her accounts, the girl's psychiatrist contacted law enforcement. Remarkably, the details provided in the dreams aligned with the unresolved murder case of the donor. This breakthrough led to the identification and eventual arrest of the murderer, who later confessed to the crime.

The case is frequently cited as evidence of cellular memory, illustrating the possibility that the heart may carry more than just blood—it may carry fragments of the soul's experiences and emotional imprint.

The concept of cellular memory suggests that organs, particularly the heart, carry memories, emotions, and preferences that can influence the recipient after a transplant. While this phenomenon remains anecdotal and not fully understood, it has been explored in research and writings, including those by the HeartMath Institute.

The HeartMath Institute's research highlights the heart's intricate neural network, which contains approximately forty thousand neurons capable of learning, memory, and emotional processing. The idea of the heart as a center of coherence—an energetic bridge between mind, body, and spirit—further fuels the interest in extraordinary cases like the one above.

While such cases are rare and often met with skepticism, they challenge our scientific understanding of consciousness, the heart, and memory. The heart's capacity to influence behavior and perception beyond its physical function opens fascinating possibilities for exploring how our bodies store and transmit information. Whether through its neural network, biochemical pathways, or energetic field, the heart may indeed play a far greater role in the story of human coherence and connection.

All of this research agrees: When the heart and mind are aligned, we enter a unique state of "outer intention," where reality shifts in our favor without excessive effort, just as we discussed in previous chapters. This alignment allows us to move smoothly toward our goals as if reality itself is supporting us.

Ritual: Connecting with Your Heart

Connect with your heart using this ritual.

- Place your hand on the heart and take ten deep breaths.
- Try breathing *from* the heart, as if your face and awareness are in the heart instead of the mind.
- Once you start to feel your nervous system relax, breathe into it a little deeper, and ask yourself a question, like "What is my heart trying to tell me right now?".

What Does the Right Path Look Like?

So how do you achieve this state? The first step is listening to the heart's desires. Ask yourself: *Do I truly want this, or do I think I should want it? Do I want it because it will make other people happy?* If a goal feels forced, it likely originates from external expectations rather than inner truth.

The second step is calming the mind's doubts. The mind will always find reasons why something isn't possible, but these doubts are often based on fear, not reality.

Instead of fighting them, acknowledge them and refocus on the heart's pull. Finally, remember the teachings of code #3 and let go of excessive attachment. The more you obsess over an outcome, the more resistance you create. When you trust in the process and release the need to control everything, reality will flow smoothly.

To circle back on the origin story of my first film, when I was in NYC a little over fifteen years ago, I had just graduated from business school, was working in the corporate world, and in the evenings, I would moonlight at film school. Our teacher often commended me for my work, and all the classes and homework lit me up from my core. I knew that I was meant to be a filmmaker or storyteller in some capacity. And it was only about ten years later that I really started to create different types of mediums in the storytelling space and received some recognition outside the classroom.

When anything lights you up or gives you so much excitement that you can't stop thinking about it or working on it, this is an excellent cue that you're on the right path. I believe that our feelings of joy, excitement, curiosity, and passion are clues for us to pay attention to. To create from the heart, we must seek paths that feel inspiring to us, without any attachment to the outcome.

And similarly, when we have feelings of contraction, heaviness, and disinterest, we're likely not aligned with the person, place, or thing at hand, or we haven't yet made sense of what it means with respect to our own life values. Ignoring the heart's guidance can lead to inner discomfort, misalignment, and misdirection, as the mind, influenced by fear and control, often overrides the heart, steering us toward unfulfilling pursuits.

When your heart is leading you, you will be carried by the winds of good fortune. You will meet the right people, who will help you get to where you need to get to. The path will likely not make any linear sense, and yet, you'll find an abundance of ease in the process.

When we have heart and mind coherence, we will move into a higher frequency state; the people we meet, the opportunities we have, and the overall vibe will feel lighter and easier. And yet—we can easily get distracted and fall into lower frequency states. I'll tell you more about how to avoid that in later chapters.

Once I became more intuitive and started following the warmth and expansion from my heart, my productivity and overall happiness and quality of life improved exponentially. I stopped wasting my time with people, places, and things that weren't resonant with my frequency. I started to meet the right people at the right time, embracing synchronicity and trusting that the Universe would provide what I desired. Aligning this faith in my heart with my logical and analytical mind became a unique superpower. I learned how to live in the moment and use logic and trust my intuition.

It's important to note that further productivity doesn't mean achieving more output. To me, productivity is about working on a project as an integrated whole being, where you can create from a space of flow rather than through willpower or sacrifice. This type of productivity allows me to continue to persevere in the long term without sacrificing a part of myself.

How we achieve our goals is more important than *if* we achieve our goals. I think many of us can remember goals that we so badly wanted to achieve, only to feel burnt out and drained after accomplishing them. The total input and output of the energy expenditure can easily end up as a net negative in the long run, and that matters when we look at our life holistically. When we burn out, we are unable to move forward until we can fully recharge. For some people, burnout leads to years and even decades of anger and resentment and stagnation. So the goal isn't everything; pay attention to how you achieve it.

There were so many moments in my life, especially in my younger years, when I made decisions that seemed rational but were ultimately at the expense of an intuitive knowing and heart-based wisdom.

Of course, this is why we need both the intuitive heart expansion *and* the mind when making decisions, but our dominant culture conditions us to privilege the logical over the intuitive. I often will use my heart and intuition as a CEO and compass when making a decision, and if it feels good, then I'll consider the rational and the logical. We need both but not at the expense of each other. When both are in harmony, we know we're making a choice that is in alignment with our greatest desires.

After years of studying with the masters of intuition through reading, courses, and lectures, I decided to go all in and earned a master certification in intuition medicine in an eighteen-month program in California.

After I started to work with both my intellect and my intuition, the course of my life changed forever. I went from managing one career that was not fulfilling to operating as if I cloned five versions of myself and created multiple careers that allowed me to express my full self, from screenwriting and podcasting to becoming an author.

So as you can see, the passions and goals in my heart of hearts led me to being able to fully embrace and enjoy my life and my career. In the words of one of my podcast guests, Viola Rose, "We have everything we need inside of ourselves. The distractions of the external world are there to keep us from looking within, but the heart holds the answers."

So, what does your heart have to say to you? What are some things you want to create based on your heart? And if there is still some nagging guilt or anxiety coming up in your self-talk when you attempt to listen to your heart, then this next chapter on changing how you think about and speak to yourself should come in handy.

CHAPTER 8

Code #8: Recast Your Inner Critic As Your Inner Coach

What are you saying within yourself right now? That is more important than anything you will ever say outwardly.

—Neville Goddard

Neo enters the virtual dojo. The glossy floor, sparring mats, and mirrored void of the program are simple and quiet, an intentionally pared-down space for learning. Morpheus stands opposite him, calm and deliberate. He tells Neo to fight him. Neo rushes at Morpheus but it's clear that he's anxious, calculating, watching for what will happen next. He tries technique, tests moves, and repeatedly fails to land a clean hit.

Morpheus interrupts the pattern. He cuts through Neo's strategizing and doubt and returns the lesson to identity. With measured intensity, he tells Neo that it is not about trying to be something; it is about *being* it in the mind and the body. He coaches Neo away from analysis and into certainty. Morpheus' instruction is blunt: "Don't think you are. Know you are."

Neo tries again, but the real turning point is not a new technique; it is the removal of the inner debate. As Neo stops arguing with himself and inhabits the skill with inner conviction, his body follows. Suddenly, moves that once seemed impossible become possible within the program. The training space responds to Neo's internal shift.

We've examined how what you identity with, you become with code #4. We've also discussed having agency over your feelings with code #5, as well as how to better balance listening to your heart and mind with code #7. A crucial consideration with all of these rules is this: How do you talk to yourself? Are you kind? Are you hard on yourself? Many of us spend our time purely reacting to our world from the perspective of an inner critic rather than from an inner coach. So, let's talk about our pesky inner conversations and inner narrators, as well as the importance of choosing whose emotions and beliefs are allowed into your own energy.

Inner Narrator

All of us have an inner narrator with whom we converse all day long. These conversations are not meaningless chatter; they matter more than almost anything that you physically do in the outer world. I often ask my clients before we start working together to take an inventory of their inner narrator. It's a revealing exercise — most people realize their thoughts feel like a wild animal, running unchecked without direction or purpose. In many cases, that voice doesn't feel like an ally at all, but more like an opponent on the other side of the field.

People often make the great mistake of attempting to change their external world instead of (or before) dealing with their inner narrator. What they don't realize is how influential our inner voice is—it can behave as a coach or best friend, or it can be our biggest critic and—in some cases—our greatest enemy. It already has an accepted identity in our culture as a negative inner voice, and therapists have even come to describe it as "the inner critic." I spoke to psychologist, neurologist, and writer Ethan Kross on *Gateways to Awakening* about the inner critic, which is the unconscious part of you that constantly is aware of and evaluates your actions, shames you, and makes you feel inferior and unworthy. It's not just imposter syndrome, though it can look a great deal like that—self-inflicted low self-esteem.

Ethan Kross, who specializes in emotional regulation, studies the "voice in our head" and how small shifts in the *way* we talk to ourselves (not only the content) can reliably change our feelings, decisions, and performance. His work blends lab experiments, field studies, and practical tools he popularized in his book *Chatter: The Voice in Our Head, Why It Matters, and How to Harness It.* One of his best-supported techniques is *distanced self-talk,* which is when you refer to yourself by name or "you" when reflecting. That small linguistic shift increases psychological distance and reduces emotional intensity, making problem-solving calmer and more rational.

He also suggests temporal distancing and rituals. Imagining how you'll feel about a problem weeks or months from now (temporal distancing) and using consistent rituals (scripts, expressive writing) interrupt automatic loops and help the nervous system "finish" the episode rather than replay it.

But what would happen if that inner voice became our best friend, cheering us on and having our back? What would happen if our inner narrator acted as our coach instead, gently connecting us to a higher and greater version of ourselves by teaching us to see and trust in the good things all around us and in our future? What if our inner voice was our cheerleader, our biggest advocate, and our champion?

We must direct the flow of energy by controlling our inner world. Neville Goddard often wrote about our "inner conversations" as the key to unlocking a different life. He believed that if we could shift how we speak to ourselves internally, we could drastically shift our lives. Like Goddard, I believe that our inner conversations set the tone for how we show up in the world.

Remember code #4: What you identify with, you become—the power of shifting your self-concept, which causes reality to respond and shift to meet your new identity and self-concept. But this is where the importance of code #8 comes in: Even if we decide to adopt a new self-concept, our inner narrator is often filled with doubt or uncertainty, so it compromises our ability to resonate with higher feeling states. The negative energy of niggling doubt and uncertainty, if not outright criticism and cruelty, cancels the positive energy of moving in the direction of a set intention or goal.

I believe that if we can connect our inner narrator to a specific identity of self *without* any negative internal reactions or emotions, we can *become* the higher frequency state relatively quickly. Shifting your identity of self is not an intellectual exercise—a lot of people understand this exercise, but hardly anyone takes the time to practice new identities and thoughts. Not everyone has the capacity to shift their inner conversations, as it requires persistence and trust that all will be well, especially when the outer world is showing you the opposite of your desire or aim.

Sometimes we have to start with overpowering our inner narrator.

"*Stop*," we might say to it. "I'm done with that version of my story."

Then, ask yourself: "What do I want instead? What would my inner coach say to me to see a different possibility, image, or thought?"

Like many others, I used to believe that my inner narration would react to the environment and the people around me, but it's actually the other way around. Still, there are people that I've met who don't even think of this relationship—from outward appearances, they appear successful, yet in reality, they have a really negative relationship with their inner voice, causing them constant stress and discontent. The lesson? Your inner narrator is not something to let run wildly amok. The world is a mirror (code #6), so once we change our inner conversations, our physical space and environments will also change. However, until then, there are many things that influence our inner conversations.

Negative Influences

Since we are now consumed by screens like our laptops, phones, and TVs all day long—not to mention the beast known as social media—showing us what to think and feel, we have lost much of our agency and sense of free will in deciding our identities, thoughts, inner conversations, and how to feel. And due to our ancestral programming of expecting danger at every turn and constantly ready to react with our fight or flight instincts, we're wired to worry and extrapolate. So, in our modern day where we are so strongly affected and influenced by technology and media and because we live in a world where we attract what we resonate with, whatever we are convinced to worry about online will only attract more reasons to worry in our lives.

Rather than zoom out and see the big picture of their own life, many people instead react and respond exclusively to the external stimuli in other's life movies, refusing to take control of their own actions and scripts. So many people live like this—blindly—that I bet if you were to listen to a random person's inner conversations, you'd find nothing but a rampage of nonsensical and non sequitur thoughts, and often ones that are very critical. For most of my life, until I understood that I could write my own life's movie, I, too, have been locked into other people's movies. And most people's movies are not even *Lifetime* specials; they're often filled with neurotic characters, insane decisions, and unfavorable plot twists.

Since we're all watching a "movie" as part of the human experience, we are often not aware that we're playing in someone else's movie until some catastrophe happens in our own life, which returns our attention back to our own movie. Some kind of mental or physical ailment is usually a leading signal that catalyzes a return to their own movie, but you can also choose to return to your own movie as well. You can decide to no longer put the same level of importance on other people's opinions either online or in person, and no longer allow yourself and your inner voice to be influenced by others and media. With work, your inner critic *can* become your inner friend rather than a voice built of everyone else's opinions and criticisms.

Now, it's only human nature to want to be accepted by others. But there is a line that should not be crossed, and unfortunately, there are many people who will do or say anything to be accepted to the point of being inauthentic and dishonest, ultimately betraying themselves just so that they won't be abandoned by their social circle. They often keep themselves small because they want to fit in, or they only look at the past as an indicator for the future, all but ensuring that they will not thrive due to reality being a mirror.

When someone dims their light or makes themselves small so they take up less space, they are living from a collapsed inner state. In our modern culture, we're indoctrinated to believe that we must fit into the values of the mainstream culture in order to fit in—go to college, get married, have two and a half kids, or be financially successful and live in a specific type of house by X age, the list goes on —and so many people do not have the courage to live from a new state with an inner conversation that is aligned with their true desires. Until you get a deep handle over your inner conversations, you will be susceptible to other people's desires and projections of you, ultimately creating an imbalanced and chaotic inner state.

Fixing Your Inner State

Our inner conversations are also great indicators that tell us which inner "state" we are in. We're always occupying an inner state, so it's worth investigating what sort of state that is. If you want to know the state of consciousness you occupy, start writing down your inner conversations. If you do so, consider what emotional themes your inner conversations are centered around. Our inner state can range anywhere from confident to desperate, acting as an emotional lens through which we experience reality. Similar to some of the lessons of the other rules we've gone over so far, your life is simply a projection of the state you are dwelling in most often.

Ritual: Getting to Know Your Inner Narrator

You can try this ritual to see what your inner narrator sounds like. Are they a critic or a coach? If you end up feeling triggered or your energy scatters as you do this ritual, then try a grounding exercise and come back when you feel ready.

1. Write down your five most frequent negative thoughts. Consider which situations trigger each negative thought and jot a couple of these down that come to mind. (Example: "I am not enough.")

2. Give every negative thought a short, believable inner coach pep talk in the present tense. (Example: "That's no way to talk to yourself! You always do your best, and that is enough.")

3. Now, rewrite your negative thoughts as positive thoughts that you'd like to have instead. (Example: "I do my best, and that is enough.")

4. Pick one tiny micro-action that aligns with the coach line, do it today, and repeat the reading. (Example: Do a chore you've been putting off this week.) For the next week, read your positive thoughts each morning, sitting with them for at least thirty seconds.

5. Separately, who is one person in your life who wishes the best for you? Could they be your accountability partner in this process? I would encourage you to ask them

to see the highest and best version of you while you're expanding.

Leaving our inner thoughts and inner state to chance in a world that is filled with every distraction available is a road leading to a mediocre and uneventful life where we are reacting to our life rather than actively creating it.

Thankfully, inner states are malleable and easy to fix. Personally, I spent three years working with my inner voice so that it would become my coach, my best friend, and the most intimate partnership I could ever have. And from that place, my external reality shifted tremendously.

To change your inner state to one that is aligned with your desires in life, you must fully operate as if you already have what you desire—as if you are already happy, fulfilled, content. Keep this peace in your mind and move through the world within this inner state and really connect with the sensory organ perception of that state. What do you taste, touch, smell, and hear? Does your aligned inner state come with a visual?

Creating a powerful new inner state alone is not enough—consistency and persistence are what bring the state to life. Many people can work on a new inner state, but without that consistency, their energy becomes scattered, and as a result, their external world loses momentum.

The truth is, most people quit working on a new inner state too soon. They abandon their creative potential because they don't see immediate results. But success is never instant—it's the result of clarity, persistence, and an unwavering commitment to the vision of your new life. If you studied the journeys of the world's most accomplished people, you'd realize how long they spent refining their craft before breaking through.

Dolly Parton wrote hundreds of songs, and only a few became hits. Tim Ferriss and Joe Rogan didn't start as global podcast leaders. They built their platforms over ten to twenty years before reaching mainstream success. They persisted, and they were committed to their vision.

Most people give up as soon as they face a single setback. As a seasoned podcaster, and after hearing about many podcasters giving up after less than a year, I know this well.

The world reflects back your level of certainty and persistence. If you hesitate, second-guess, or waver in your commitment, you will receive uncertain results in return. If your new inner state isn't working, ask yourself—at what moment did I stop fully choosing it? When people ask how long it takes, I often reply with, "As long as it takes to no longer have any doubt, and you detach from the outcome."

I've also found that confusion is one of the worst states to be in. A lack of clarity is the real reason most people don't get results. If you are confused about what you want to create or why you're creating it, your reality will reflect that confusion. Avoid people who are always "confused" as they are usually a huge waste of energy. Confused people often don't spend enough time alone and hang onto others like anchors and often judge them for their own level of confusion.

So here's a challenge: Decide right now to be absolutely certain and committed. Then wait and see how the mirror reflects your commitment back to you. Because the ones who get what they want long-term aren't always the most talented—they're the ones who simply refuse to stop. They are *certain*. When you doubt yourself, you allow others to reflect that doubt back. So do not doubt yourself! It's only an invitation for others to question yourself.

The Law of Entrainment

Regarding others, remember the theory that we are the sum of the five people we are closest to that I mentioned in chapter 3? Well, it's a similar concept here: Who we spend time with each day matters when it comes to our inner states. If you want to know your future state, look at your five closest friends—not just at their personalities but their incomes, habits, mindsets, relationships, and even health. Because whether you realize it or not, you are entraining their energy—syncing up with their frequencies, their beliefs, and their limitations.

With roots in physics, the Law of Entrainment states that things that vibrate or have rhythm patterns, even if those are different patterns at the start, will eventually sync up with each other when in the presence of one another. It happens everywhere:

- Grandfather clocks in the same room will synchronize their pendulums.
- Women living together often experience synchronized menstrual cycles.

- Some species of fish and even birds group together in synchronized, hypnotic patterns, such as in starling murmurations.

This law affects us too. Think of how our nervous systems naturally calibrate to the people we're around, whether they're stressed and chaotic or calm and expansive. And it's not just energy—it's cold, hard numbers.

For instance, you are likely to earn an average of your five closest friends. If your best friend becomes obese, your chances of becoming obese increase by 57 percent. You're also 45 percent more likely to smoke if a friend smokes, and your divorce risk increases by 75 percent if your close friends are divorcing. So, your environment is shaping you whether you like it or not. We are always exchanging energy with the people and environments around us.

So, consider this question: Are you being shaped into your highest potential or into someone else's limitations?

I've also noticed that most people, whether they realize it or not, are constantly transferring their fear onto others—offloading their anxieties, doubts, and insecurities as a weight for someone else to carry. This is called "emotional contagion." Emotional contagion occurs when one person's emotions unconsciously affect another's energy. For example, think about how you feel when you enter a busy airport versus a church or sacred place, or how walking into a tense room can instantly make you feel uneasy, just as being around a joyful person can elevate your mood without a word being spoken.

In my experience, the most dangerous kind of connection, besides someone who is confused, is with someone who subtly inserts doubt into your field, even by accident.

I know many people who respond to someone else's exciting news with fear, doubt, or criticism. Maybe you're chatting with a friend or coworker and share something meaningful—like trying to get pregnant—and instead of celebrating with you, they bring up your age, statistics, or worst-case scenarios. Other times, it's even more subtle: a raised eyebrow, an eye-roll, a moment of hesitation wrapped in silence.

The same is true for any new creative project you might be working on. That tiny seed of doubt, which is often disguised as concern or realism, can quietly unravel your confidence in your own dreams, causing you to stop reaching for them at all.

It's subtle but powerful.

Most people haven't yet graduated from emotional-intelligence kindergarten. They will unconsciously project or transfer their fears onto others without pausing to ask themselves why. Don't let their skepticism and negative energy stop you. Share your visions with those who expand your field—not those who contract it.

Protect your dreams. Choose your audience wisely.

Of course, I believe we all need to develop energetic resilience so other people's energy doesn't impact us (remember the lesson in chapter 1 on building resilience?)—but it's also easier not to walk through fire just to prove we can. Choose to build your life with those who see you clearly and celebrate your becoming. This is a form of faith—faith in our values and faith in the kinds of people and environments we surround ourselves with, not to mention faith in ourselves.

In every moment, you are choosing between fear and faith. There is no neutral ground. Faith is the highest currency. Fear, on the other hand, is a weight—a debt that drains energy, creativity, and possibility.

Your ability to remain unmoved by fear—your ability to hold your own energetic ground—is your greatest power.

And finally, no one is responsible for maintaining your own level of faith and certainty in yourself other than you. It is something many of us need to work on everyday. These days, I rarely leave the house without connecting to that feeling of trust in myself first.

If you can hold faith in yourself, in your vision, and in the unseen when others around you are unraveling, you'll become unbreachable. You'll stop absorbing the limitations of those around you. You'll remain resilient, clear, and unshakable.

When you no longer allow other's negative energy to affect you, you'll be better prepared and able to befriend your inner narrator and choose which inner conversations hold true value. That's when the people, opportunities, and spaces that match and resonate with your inner world will be drawn to you. I also believe that the reason why most people don't get what they want in life is because of other people's negative projections through the consistent feedback of doubt and confusion. And I know that the opposite is also true. If you have even one person, perhaps a mentor, who sees your potential, they will help expand your imagination toward the greatest next version of yourself. That has been the case in my own life.

I've been blessed to have met countless mentors who saw my potential. One of my mentors said to me in my early thirties, "Yasmeen, I've never met someone with your skill set and capacity." I was so bewildered when she said this because I had simply never seen myself that way. She always saw me as someone who could do anything. And because of her, I started to disconnect (at first slowly) from the matrix. I realized that just her belief in a new possibility for me was all I needed as a reference point to reach for a greater version of myself.

Embracing code #8 does wonders to help set you up to better communicate with your inner coach as well as letting the Universe know what sort of things and people you want to invite into your life . Next, we'll look at ways to help you literally rewrite your identity and recreate your life.

CHAPTER 9

Code #9: Intention, Prayer, and Future-Self Scripting

Scripting isn't about writing a to-do list — it's about stepping into the identity of the person who already experiences the result you're aiming for.

—Royce Christyn

Looking back on his journey in *The Matrix*, Neo was rewriting his identity, shifting into a new self-concept, and stepping into his future reality.

That's exactly how intention, prayer, and future-self scripting work. And once Neo knew he was The One, reality had no choice but to reflect that truth.

In this chapter, we'll examine code #9, which focuses on consciously creating your life through intention, prayer, and future-self scripting. By directing your energy, attention, and awareness from a future-state, you can lock into a new reality, a new timeline, and a new sense of self. We'll start with the foundation of code #9, intention, which has been alluded to in many of the previous chapters.

Intention

At the Academy of Intuition Medicine, we learned that "energy follows thought." And this is essentially what an intention is, a directive that allows energy to move in a specific direction. Once you have a thought (for example, *I intend to speak on stage at The Moth*), you send a flurry of energy in that direction. Another way to think about an intention is that it's similar to goal setting, except an intention is a directive with implied action. One has to explicitly state "I intend" in their request.

Many people live their life without setting a single intention. Can you imagine that? If you don't set an intention, I can guarantee you'll be living out other people's intentions.

Intention is one of the most accessible ways to direct the flow of energy in your favor and toward what you prefer or desire. Think about intention as the dial on your radio. Whichever way you choose to direct your dial, your energy will flow.

When intention is set within a loving partnership, it carries even more power. The late Brenda Dunne, who managed the Princeton Engineering Anomalies Research (PEAR) Lab from 1979 to 2007, found that intention was dramatically amplified when practiced by emotionally bonded pairs. In other words, setting an intention with someone you're deeply connected to doesn't just double the energy—it supercharges it.

Specifically, when romantic couples worked together on influencing random event generators (REGs), the effects were more pronounced compared to individuals or non-bonded pairs. (If you haven't heard of REGs, they are devices that give completely random binary numbers.) This finding suggests that emotional resonance—being on the same level, the same wavelength, the same frequency—between partners may amplify the interaction between consciousness and physical systems. So, it can be very beneficial if you and a loved one have the same goal that you're working toward to put your minds together and send an intention out into the Universe, then wait for the Universe to reflect your combined energy back at you.

Segment Intending & Asking Better Questions

Sometimes it's helpful to energetically align with what you want to create before stepping into it. This is where "segment intending" comes into play. Segment intending is the practice of setting a clear intention for a specific part of your day or a specific experience. For example, you might say something simple like: "I intend to have a grounded, focused morning," "I intend for this meeting to be collaborative and inspiring," or "I intend to feel calm and energized during this conversation."

Segment intending brings presence into the moments we usually rush through. It helps us become conscious creators of our experience of life rather than reacting on autopilot.

Another powerful approach to segment intending is through the use of *questions as intention*. Have you noticed how we tend to ask ourselves disempowering questions instead of empowering ones? Some examples are: "Why do I always get stuck in traffic?" and "Why do I have such bad luck when going on dates?". Instead of accidentally intending what you *don't* want, you can reorient your energy by asking questions like: "Why do I always have such amazing mornings?" or "Why do my meetings flow so effortlessly?" or "Why am I always so supported?". Asking questions that point out positive things in your life instead of negative things opens up space for possibility and primes your mind to find evidence that supports the reality you want to create. These kinds of questions open space for possibility and prime your mind to find evidence of the reality you *actually* want to create.

The Placebo Effect: The Power of Belief

Even if you are not interested in setting intentions, the placebo effect is one of the most important things to understand when it comes to belief.

What you believe, your body and mind will be influenced and will often make what you believe *real*.

The placebo effect proves that belief alone can create physical changes in the body. Patients given sugar pills but told they were receiving medicine can experience real healing—because their mind and body align with the expectation of healing. I'm not offering medical advice— the science is complex and ongoing—but it's humbling to witness how conviction and expectation can alter an experience.

When you set a strong intention, your brain and body begin to rearrange themselves as if your desired outcome is already happening, increasing the likelihood that you'll experience it. However, there are two ways to pray that could also be helpful in setting your intention.

Invocation & Prayer

I wish I could have a baby. I wish I could get a promotion. I wish I had just a little extra money this month. In a sense, we are always praying, but we're praying with little energy. We are praying from a place of lack, of scarcity.

A prayer is not a wish. A prayer is a directive, a command, an invocation to call in a specific set of energetic initiatives. A prayer is usually done with focus, energy, and a sense of strength.

Prayer is powerful. Prayer is taking intention a step further. Prayer, in my opinion, is setting a directed field of intention in motion. Many people who grew up in an orthodox or religious household might cringe at the mention of prayer. If that's you, that's okay. Or maybe the concept of using prayer in this way is welcome. The idea here is that you can create your own prayer, for whatever it is that you want.

People often joke that they only pray when calamity strikes in their life. But prayer is an underdeveloped and underrated tool. What do you have to lose? I always wonder why people don't use their words to call in what they want, instead spending so much time using their words to complain about things that they don't want.

There are so many powerful prayers from different spiritual traditions. If you don't know any, I would suggest creating your own prayer and finding what works for you. Here is an example of a prayer I created and one I use often: *In the name of the Most High, I command that all negative and dissonant energy be released and transmuted into unconditional love. Thank you, it is done.*

Here is another one I created for health, since many clients and friends have asked:

Invocation for Health and Embodiment

In the Name of the Most High,
Infinite Intelligence that breathes through all forms,
In the name of the Most High, I open now to the divine
template of radiant health,
Perfect, whole, and holy.

I call forth the original blueprint of my body,
the divine design encoded in light, untouched by distortion,
restored now by the Grace of Creation.

I invite the Universal Presence into every cell,
every organ, every bone,
every river and rhythm of my being.
Let all systems align now with Truth,
with vitality, with the sacred memory of wholeness.

In this moment, I release all contracts, stories, and timelines
that no longer serve my wellness.
I dissolve the residue of dis-ease,
transmute the frequencies of pain, depletion, and imbalance.
They are no longer needed. I choose differently now.

I call upon the Angels of Healing,
the Guides of Regeneration,
the Elders of Divine Embodiment,
to walk with me now.

May my blood sing with vitality.
May my breath return me to presence.
May my spine hold me like the Tree of Life itself.

May my body become a temple of joyful movement,
a sanctuary of the soul.

Thank you, Great Spirit,
for restoring my system to Divine Harmony.
Thank you for anchoring this healing in all dimensions—past,
present, and future.
Thank you for my strong, supple, and sovereign body.

And so it is.

Here is another example of a prayer I created and one I use to remove stagnant or negative energy:

In the name of the Most High, I command that all negative energy leaves my physical body, mental body, emotional body across all time, space, and dimension.

Prayer can also be done by giving gratitude for whatever it is you want from a future stance, or in other words, future-scripting. For example, one way to pray is to ask for something out of lack. And the other way is to pray with gratitude for whatever you desire already being true. Here is an example.

- **Old prayer (lack-based thinking):** "God, please give me this job. I really want it." This implies separation and doubt, coming to the point of intention from a negative perspective.

- **Future-self prayer (abundance-based thinking):** "I am grateful that I am already thriving in my dream job. I love my work, and I feel deeply fulfilled and grateful." This method uses a positive approach by assuming the goal of the intention is already accomplished or has been reached.

Being grateful for what you have and what you will have is important because it signals to the Universe who you are and what you are resonating with.

Ritual: Praying in Action

In this ritual, you can practice creating your own prayer and figuring out what works for you. Start out with something simple:

1. Commit to starting each day with a prayer that makes you smile. Perhaps you can create one to two sentences that would be meaningful for you.

2. If you're stuck, try something as simple as "I intend to have a beautiful and wonderful day."

How'd that go for you? Feel free to stick to that first prayer for now and come back for the second part of this ritual later. Next, see if you can come up with a future-self prayer, acting from the stance that you already have what you desire and you are simply giving gratitude for your abundance:

1. Consider these questions: What do you want to experience in this lifetime? Who and what do you want to call in? How about your higher self or a higher version of yourself?

2. Now, write a future-self prayer (perhaps writing it in your journal) that gives gratitude for what you see yourself already having. It can be as long or as short as you'd like.

3. Revisit this prayer for the next few days or weeks, praying it into existence.

Future-Self Scripting

What does it mean to live from the end state?

I have always been an avid writer and wrote about my inner world in some kind of physical journal or online diary in every era of my life with some long stretches of silence. I still remember looking at my pink-paged diary with green writing lines from when I was seven years old. I would address it as "Dear Diary," and then sign off by saying "Bye," as if I were signing off to a trusted friend. I felt like I could tell the diary all of the most intimate details of my life that I could tell no one else.

About a decade ago, I discovered Julia Cameron's book, *The Artist's Way*, and her famous Morning Pages exercise, which is a simple yet powerful practice of writing three pages of free-flowing thoughts each day. I kept this going for over a decade, and it produced some profound revelations in my life.

Whenever I stopped journaling, I would often notice that my own life would stall and my sense of inner knowing would slow down. I soon realized that writing was a non-negotiable medicine for my soul and that I needed it to sustain me in my life.

A few years ago, I took my journaling practice a step further. I started the practice of future-self scripting, a manifestation technique where you write a detailed narrative, in the present tense, of your desired future as if it has already happened.

At first, I thought it was absurd. Writing about a future reality as if it were already true? It felt like wishful thinking. But I committed to it anyway, and soon, the results were undeniable.

One powerful example happened in my life in February of 2022. I had created a ten-part audio episodic miniseries, *Hyphenated Journey*, and my team submitted it to Apple Podcasts.

Every single day, I wrote in my journal: "I am so grateful to be recognized by Apple and featured at the top of Apple Podcast's carousel." For most podcasters, this level of visibility is near impossible, but it's a tremendous honor. To be given the real estate of the top of the Apple carousel has pretty low statistical chances overall. Day after day, I would write about how grateful I was, while also dropping importance.

Weeks later, my team called to tell me that not only did Apple select *Hyphenated Journey* to their carousel, they had promoted it to the top of the carousel. I looked on Apple Podcasts—and there it was.

So, what is future-self scripting? Let's dive in.

On my seasonal podcast *Gateways to Awakening*, I sat down with author Royce Christyn, where we spoke about his scripting method and its scientific foundations from his book, *Scripting the Life You Want: Manifest Your Dreams with Just Pen and Paper*. In his book, he explores how this technique aligns with principles from quantum mechanics and neuroscience.

He discusses that by scripting—literally writing things down—desired outcomes as if they have already occurred, individuals may impact the probabilities of these events manifesting in their lives. He specifically highlights the role of the reticular activating system (RAS), a network in the brain that filters sensory information and influences what we pay attention to, as being a key element in the success of scripting. By consistently scripting and focusing on specific goals, individuals can program their RAS to notice opportunities and resources that align with their desires, thereby enhancing them. In other words, by scripting about your ideal future, you train your mind to notice and act on opportunities that align with your vision.

During our interview, he created a "test" with the RAS. He asked me which superhero was my favorite when I was a kid, and I admittedly said, "Michelangelo from *Teenage Mutant Ninja Turtles*." He said that I would see an image or hear of something related to Michaelangelo in the coming weeks. I admit, I was perplexed because it was 2023, and I didn't know of anyone who spoke about Michaelangelo anymore, let alone someone who cared about the *Teenage Mutant Ninja Turtles.* It just does not normally come up in conversation. But sure enough—it did! A few weeks later, I was invited to a *Teenage Mutant Ninja Turtle* theme party with Michaelangelo on the cover.

Here's another general example of future-self scripting: "I am so grateful that my company is thriving. Every day, I receive messages from people telling me how much my work has impacted them. I wake up feeling excited, knowing that I am living my highest purpose. Opportunities flow to me effortlessly, and I am surrounded by supportive, inspiring people who uplift me."

Obviously, you'll want to make it more specific than this example, but this is a great generic future-self script to start with if you don't know how to begin. And you can always practice intention by intending that this future-self script or something better can reveal itself to you.

The words that we speak to ourselves and about what is possible matter. Many people are unaware that the words they use to describe their life and their future likely make quite an impact on that future.

Ritual: Self-Scripting Your Future

Words are powerful tools of creation. In scripting, you are not just writing for the sake of it; you are consciously shaping your reality with your words.

To practice, let's fast forward to a year from now. Start writing about this last year and share your highlight reel about what's happened: events, opportunities, health, relationships, romance, where you live, etc. What good things are you future-scripting for this year?

This is such a fun ritual; it gives you the opportunity to think about what you want, and, as a bonus, it often immediately changes the inner state that you're in. The reticular activating system (RAS) is truly one's guide to directing the flow of energy toward a future that you desire rather than focusing on what you don't want.

We've learned how to focus our inner energy—to script our future selves, reframe the inner critic, and hold the assumption long enough for it to harden into fact. But intention alone doesn't manufacture new things; it only prepares the soil. Creativity is the daily practice that plants, tends, and harvests novel outcomes: improvisation, iteration, and playful risk-taking transform imagined futures into lived realities. In the next chapter, we'll sharpen the imaginative muscles you'll need to do that work.

CHAPTER 10

Code #10: To Remain in Harmony with the Universe, You Must Expand Along with It

Sometimes genius consists of staring out the window.
—Gertrude Stein

N eo sits in a bare, dimly lit room opposite Morpheus. Between them on a small table rests two capsules—one red, one blue—simple objects that have been turned into a hinge for everything Neo thinks he knows. Morpheus explains the choice: One pill returns you to the comfortable illusion, and the other forces you to wake to the real, uncertain world beyond the screen.

The red pill will show him the truth, however difficult.

Neo swallows the red pill. The next moments are a physical unravelling—machines, tubes, and a violent, literal unplugging from the constructed life he has accepted. He wakes into a harsher, truer world and the work of becoming, and true creativity, begins.

Like Neo choosing the red pill, this chapter focuses on expanding your known world. The Universe is constantly expanding, and you must choose to expand along with it or be left behind, stuck in the simulation. To be creative, you must expand your horizons, your perspective, of the world. As the basis for code #10, creativity is the door to true harmony, to divine expansion. Mastering your creativity and embracing it as part of your power is the last of the ten codes to master your energy, the previous of which have so far been mainly focused on honing your inner self and how you move in the world. Sharing your creativity means that you are choosing to share a part of yourself with the rest of the world, actively moving from "me consciousness" to "we consciousness," aligning with the Universe's expansive nature, and ultimately, becoming a conduit for something greater than yourself.

Creative Play

The red-pill moment is a metaphor for creative courage. Creativity starts not with tricks or shortcuts but with the willingness to choose reality honestly—to leave comfortable imitation behind and face uncertainty, failure, and learning. Choosing the red pill is choosing curiosity over comfort. That leap into the unknown is where original work is born.

I've often wondered why so many adults assume "playing" is for kids. It's so important to train our mind to lean into and use our imagination and creativity every single day! So many of us live in a pattern of predictable and repetitive thinking, rather than in possibility and play.

Everyone is creative, but children especially know how to be creative. Have you ever seen a child that doesn't play? Recently, I came back from visiting my fourteen-month-old nephew, and he is on a constant journey of adventure, all day long. Our bodies and minds are wired to play, to seek, to be curious, and to connect with that energy state all the time. Yet, many adults resign their lives to "work" and leave play out almost entirely.

I believe that playing a little bit each day (or a lot each day) is one of the most powerful ways to reconnect with our heart. Play expands our perception—it opens us up to wonder, insight, and unexpected solutions. It helps us make connections across seemingly unrelated ideas. It increases our capacity to hold paradoxes. And it makes us better humans. When we're creative, we can be more present, more joyful, and more available in our relationships.

Eric Maisel, the author of *CoachingtheArtist Within*, who I interviewed on my podcast, suggestscarving time out in the morning before you start your day to work on your creative projects. He believes that most people lose the energy and motivation to create once the day continues or once they start their "day job," and this can often lead to despondency and depression in the long term. However, we all haveslightly different circadian rhythms, and not all of ushave the bandwidth or time to play before work or in the morning. So, find a time that works for you and make it a habit to play and create at least once a day.

In my interview with Dr. Karla McLaren, an emotions and empathy expert and social science researcher, on my podcast, she said that when employees are not given creative agency at work, they will create unnecessary drama in interpersonal relationships with others in the workplace. Being able to work creatively and with agency on what lights us up is the elixir that makes life exciting. This also rings true for interpersonal relationships outside of work.

According to Dr. McLaren, emotions are data—they carry vital information about our values, boundaries, and inner alignment. So when individuals are deprived of the opportunity to work on things that energize and inspire them, those emotions (frustration, restlessness, boredom, and even grief) don't just disappear. Instead, they seek an outlet.

Without a healthy channel for creative flow, the psyche often redirects blocked energy into relational dynamics— drama, gossip, territorialism, and power struggles. This isn't necessarily because people want conflict but because they are trying to find *something* that stimulates their nervous system. Dr. McLaren warns that unacknowledged emotions like anger or envy might morph into disconnection or sabotage when they're not honored as signals for change. This is precisely why creativity is such an important part of our lives—without it, the pent-up energy seeks other outlets.

So What Exactly Is the Creative Process?

There are many parts of the creative process, like coming up with the idea, editing the idea, putting it into a structure of some sort, and packaging it so that the world can digest and metabolize it. There is also a difference between the creative process versus the output (i.e., a piece of art). For this discussion, I will focus on the process itself.

My definition of the creative process begins with the impulse I get when I am creating something that is a part of me that is aching to be released. It is the feeling I get when I'm connected to a source greater than myself when my ego gets out of the way—and it's an experience, an action, a verb more than a noun. It's the shivers I get when I am moved by something profound or by something that makes me expand my perspective in this world.

When I'm in the space of creating, it feels like I'm tapping into a field of consciousness and space that is much greater than me, a space that feels so vast and infinite, filled with mystery and primordial wisdom. When I'm connected to this field, I somehow feel safe, because I know that whatever is moving through me is greater than my small ego-self, and therefore, the invitation is always welcome.

And creativity requires that we let go of society's point of view on our creation. In Joseph Gordon-Levitt's TED Talk on creativity, he tells us that creativity is about *paying attention* rather than *getting attention*, and how craving attention makes you less creative. There is a big difference between getting attention and the rush of recognition versus paying attention, which is a deep, focused presence that is detached from the outcome. He goes on to say that when you fully engage in the creative moment and pay attention, you enter a state of flow and this produces deeper satisfaction and better work than chasing external validation. He also recommends treating other creators as collaborators rather than competitors, so you can shield one another from attention-seeking distractions and stay focused on creating things.

I think the creative process is something we have to also intentionally desire. We need to create space for new ideas to come in and make this practice a priority. Most people in modern society don't have that space, or they live so in fear and reactivity that there's no opening for them to connect with themselves in a deeper way. A defensive stance in life is not a creative life.

Many may consider a creative life to be like a fun hobby instead of a career or the side dish instead of the meal itself. This is such a tragic way of thinking though. We are so deeply in need of creating and expressing a truth within us—and this need is even stronger than our identity, but, again, people don't often understand this. A couple of common excuses for people who avoid creativity in their lives are they must "pay their bills" or they "don't have time."

But think about it this way: There is only one of you. Only one of you will exist on this planet, in your form, with your personality, expression and set of opinions and ideas. You play a part in the great symphony of the collective harmony, and we need to hear your sound. Creativity ultimately affects more than just your own life; it influences your community and society. It has the capacity to change the world.

I was taught at a young age by society not to dream outside the box or have aspirations that exceeded social norms. There were only a certain number of select professions available to me growing up, and it took me nearly a decade to course correct. See, many of us, including me for a while there, are afraid of the rejection we may face when we choose to create. It is difficult—but not impossible—to step out onto the stage, for which we've previously only ever been an audience member, and choose to create for all to see.

I also believe that creativity is non-linear and happens when we are not thinking or using logic. I think logic and intelligence are needed to ground a creative idea into form, but intelligence is limited to what has already existed and not what has yet to exist. Think about it—when have you had some of your breakthrough or aha moments? Has it been during times of intense concentration in the moment of working on a project? Or has it been when you're in the shower or meditating, on a walk in nature or some other time when you weren't actively thinking and trying to force an idea or solution? Creativity is linked to our unique ability to tap into our intuition and sit in a space of openness, trust, and acceptance of the Universe. It allows us to access the infinite.

The Second Chakra and the Wellspring of Creative Mindset

For centuries, mystics, artists, and seers have pointed to the second chakra, which sits roughly two finger-widths below the navel and two finger-widths in from the pelvic bone, as the source of fertility for ideas, desire, and creative energy. *Chakra* is a Sanskrit word that means "wheel" or "spin." In yogic anatomy, the second chakra is called

"Svādhiṣthāna," the sacral center, and when we learn to move with it rather than against it, creativity becomes less about proving ourselves and more about answering a beautiful, internal yes. This chapter is an invitation to cultivate a connection with that center.

On my podcast, I interviewed Anodea Judith, a well-known author on the chakras. In yogic traditions, Judith said, chakras are described as energetic centers that sit along the spine and help organize how life force, often called prana or energy, moves through the body. Think of them as hubs where physical sensation, emotion, identity, and attention meet. Many modern teachers pair each chakra with a major gland or organ in the endocrine system. The second chakra, the sacral asks, "Do I want this?" and "Do I feel it?" It is what supports your capacity to receive, desire, move, play, and allow form to be birthed from feeling. Creative work that leans on the sacral is curious, embodied, and willing to be messy. It trusts your impulses and is generous with time, attention, and sensuality. It doesn't rush from idea to edit; it luxuriates in the creative process.

When this center is balanced, you feel light in your pelvis, open to pleasure that is not dependent on outcomes, able to imagine wildly and return to your desk. When it is contracted, you may find yourself blocked, overly self-conscious, addicted to approval, or creatively literal—producing things that look like other people's work because it feels safer than the risk of being original. Other signs of your second chakra being blocked include emotional heaviness or numbness and compulsive habits around food, screens, or sex, as well as a persistent inability to finish projects because the risk of being seen feels unbearable.

Ritual: Water, Movement, and an Orange Altar

Below are ritual prompts and somatic tools you can utilize when you wake as well as throughout the day. You can also use these before, during, and after creative work. You'll notice the color orange is utilized often—this is because orange is the color associated with the second chakra, so these practices are designed to nourish your sacral chakra and your creativity.

- Wake with water—Drink a glass of room-temperature water with a squeeze of citrus. Water lubricates the creative tissues; citrus gives a gentle charge to the sacral center.

- Pelvic breathing (five to seven minutes)—Sit tall. Place a hand two inches below your navel. Breathe slowly into that area, feeling the belly expand toward the hand on the inhale and soften on the exhale. Imagine your breath stirring a warm orange pool in the pelvis. This is not forceful; it is an invitation.

- Hip-opening movement (seven to ten minutes)— gentle cat and cow yoga poses and slow pelvic circles. Focus on releasing tension and noticing the sensations in your body. Movement frees creative attention from constriction.

- Set an orange altar—Place one orange or water in an orange bowl near your workspace. Before you begin a creative session, touch the orange or the bowl and say silently, *I am open to receive.* This small ritual trains your nervous system to associate the sacral with permission.

When the sacral is balanced, you feel naturally curious and open to play; starting a project becomes answering an invitation rather than ticking off a checklist. You lose track of time because you can't wait to return to your work. You begin from pleasure rather than from a need for approval, and your body becomes a reliable guide. Sensations inform your choices and keep the work honest. Setbacks land softer: You recover faster because your drive is fueled by intrinsic delight, not external validation. I experienced this when writing screenplays and working on my podcast and film: I could draft 120 pages in eight days because my creative energy flowed like a waterfall from an endless source. I also felt that way whenever I was interviewing a thought-leader on my podcast. Time simply collapsed— what seemed like years passed in only a few hours.

Do Not Become Predictable

Lastly, do not become predictable. Let's face it, predictability is boring. So many people have rigidly controlled their lives to the point that there is no room for anything new, especially anything creative, to come through. I'm often perplexed at how many people don't have a relationship with their creativity and will echo other people and borrow their narratives because they don't take the space to claim what feels exciting and expansive.

I understand that long, focused practice is how mastery is born, but I've noticed a discouraging pattern: Creators will fall into developing a body of work that they repeat for years and sometimes decades. I call this copy-and-paste creativity, and over time, I've observed that boredom replaces curiosity. We need to keep updating our ideas and inviting fresh conversations into our consciousness and into the world. The easiest way to get out of monotonous thinking is to shift your awareness as much as you can so that it doesn't become stagnant or hold onto the same frame: the same coffee shop, the same walk to work, the same conversations.

What is a thought you've never had before? I suggest that you spend time inviting a new thought into your world that you are intentionally creating. Because true creativity isn't just about output — it's about aliveness. It's about staying in relationship with wonder. When you step outside the familiar frame, even slightly, you allow your perception to reorganize. That's when real insight happens. Let your creative practice be a place of discovery, not performance. Let it evolve. Let it surprise you. What you make from that place will carry the signature of the present moment, and that is where your most vital work lives.

To live by these codes is not a one-time act of insight, but a continuous unfolding. The tenth code — *To Remain in Harmony with the Universe, You Must Expand Along with It* — asks you to embody expansion as a way of life: to stay open, evolving, in movement with the living intelligence of the cosmos.

But what happens when that movement halts?

What happens when you contract — and you lose your way?

CHAPTER 11

When You Lose Your Way

Humility is not thinking less of yourself, it's thinking of yourself less.

—C. S. Lewis

The Oracle's kitchen is ordinary, and she greets Neo with something quieter than prophecy. She tells him that he is "not The One."

At first Neo's defensiveness is nearly invisible: a tightening around the throat, a small, involuntary swallow. Inside, a whole architecture tumbles: Futures he had already begun to live out in his mind collapse, and with them, a tidy sense of meaning. The belief that had been propelling him becomes a rumor; the future he was rehearsing disappears like a stage set dropped in the dark. The body narrows. He watches the possibility of destiny turn into a question mark, and the question mark lodges in his gut.

Suddenly his momentum falters: practice turns tentative, he searches for signs instead of doing the work, and doubt becomes the loudest story in the room.

In this chapter, now that we've gone over the ten energy mastery codes, we'll discuss an important lesson as you are practicing the codes and incorporating them into your life: It's common to lose your way. And that's okay. We all have this moment. What matters is that you catch yourself in time and don't let your ego once again consume you.

When the Ego Takes Hold

Your ego will try to mess with you. It waits for the perfect moment—when you're flying high, receiving accolades, and being validated for your work. It creeps in, whispering, "You are exceptional," "You are invincible," and "You are *untouchable*." Sounds great, right? Wrong. For if you're not careful, it will take you for a ride—one that disconnects you from your purpose and makes you forget why you started in the first place.

That kind of power—external recognition, status, admiration—is intoxicating, but it's a trap. Because the moment you attach your worth to validation, you lose your awareness. You start living for the approval of others rather than for the truth within you. And suddenly, before you even realize what's happening, you're further away from yourself than when you started.

Have you ever noticed how when you're doing something well, you're usually in *flow*? And when people start to compliment you or critique you, what is it that usually happens? You're often taken out of flow, and you move from using the heart to using the head. And just like when we went over code #7, relying more on the logical mind than the passionate heart can hinder, if not completely stop, your forward movement.

Let's take a closer look at this concept: What happens when you've built a high frequency life, living out your main character dreams, and you start to gain power, influence, joy, and inner peace, and you suddenly start to lose your awareness?

It could have started with something small—perhaps you have a meeting with your manager, and it doesn't go exactly as planned. Now you're starting to worry about your job, and all of a sudden, your thoughts spiral into a loop of scarcity and loss. Before you know it, you're arguing with your spouse and kids or other loved ones.

Suddenly, your thoughts start to fire in neural networks—or, as I think of them, negative neighborhoods—that are not in alignment with your higher version of self. One thing after another begins to crumble, and you start to look at your external reality as if it's a nightmare rather than your life.

We've all been there. We're in flow, aligned, perhaps even experiencing moments of *samadhi*—a deep, ecstatic connection to life itself. Everything seems to be working. Then *boom*. Something happens.

The fall.

The reckoning.

The ego inflates, and suddenly, you're faced with a version of yourself you thought you had outgrown. Maybe it's an old insecurity resurfacing or someone from your past mirroring back the very thing you swore you had transcended. Maybe it's your body, forcing you to slow down—a knee injury, an illness, a sudden disruption.

When the ego takes over, you might forget the codes that once kept you grounded. You slip back into the old patterns, the ones you thought you had left behind. You chase material success for the sake of status. You start measuring your worth by how others perceive you. You prioritize control over surrender, illusion over truth.

The opposite is also true: Staying humble, grateful, and rooted in heart-centered creativity guards you from that fall. But success can bend people in strange ways. I've noticed that many people admire someone's professional success but don't hold them accountable for their personal or emotional life—pedestalization breeds flattering dishonesty among peers, and that lack of honest feedback lets the ego distort your energy without you noticing.

The work, then, is twofold: cultivate humility and keep honest mirrors close. Practice gratitude so praise doesn't become the currency of your identity, and invite trusted people to tell you how you actually are showing up, not what you look like. That's how you stay anchored when the wind picks up.

What exactly is at stake if you just read these ten energy codes but don't *live* them? What will happen if you let your ego pull you back into default mode, into contraction instead of expansion? The cost is greater than you realize.

But it's okay. We are human, and we live in a world that is rigged against us.

It's natural to make mistakes, and I assure you, you will make them.

But instead of letting months, years, or even a lifetime go by, the goal is to catch yourself as soon as you can. Remember to not get sucked into someone else's life movie once again; you are the main character and the writer of *your* life movie.

Catching myself on this precipice used to take me months and years now takes me days and sometimes hours.

My hope is that you, too, integrate these rules and remember to return to them often. These codes are a user manual to keep you rooted in the greatest version of yourself. Remember that your value isn't determined by applause, wealth, or recognition but by your ability to remain aligned in the face of all of it.

This is the real work: staying awake, staying aware, and not letting the ego pull you into a more negative space than where you started. Because if you're not conscious of it, that's exactly where it will take you.

Catching Yourself in Time

So let's say you're on a negative spiral—but this time, you caught yourself. You became aware of your ego's proud head rising up. Like Neo, you wake up!

You decide to have a good laugh at the situation and remember that you are the director of your life's movie. And it is a divine comedy where everyone is an actor playing a role in your life to help you understand yourself.

The ego likes to play the game of win and lose, shadow and light, right and wrong, better and worse. When you're complaining or judging about something or someone, you can be sure: Your ego has taken the reins over your awareness.

When you do get hooked into a negative mindset, the most valuable thing you can do is create an instant shift. Take radical action and move immediately into a state of gratitude. If you need to, delete your social media apps and any other kind of media that will keep you locked in negative mindsets and negative inner conversations. One way to immediately shift off these lower frequency life tracks and negative thought loops is to keep a journal and label it "Wins" or "Gratitude." John Demartini, one of my guests on *Gateways to Awakening*, said that he tracks his daily wins at the end of each day and has done so for over fifty years! Demartini describes the habit as foundational, helping him to stay focused on his mission, notice incremental progress, and reinterpret challenges as fuel for growth. When you focus on what you want, you get more of what you want. So, start to track your small wins and what you're grateful for. It's really that simple.

Before I fully knew all of these codes, I found myself in a negative spiral right after a big win in 2017. I was flying high off the success of the short film I wrote, which later was selected into eight film festivals. I had also just published my first book, and it had done well.

A few weeks after both of these accomplishments, and celebrating them at a party, I got into a terrible accident on an electric bike in San Francisco. I remember it like it was yesterday. I flew off a hill after braking on a cable car track. My bike flew through the air, and I broke my ribs and tore my ACL and MCL. This was no small accident; it left me bruised and injured so badly that I was on crutches for months. Over the following six months, my body became a liability rather than an asset.

Looking back now, I believe that my ego had gotten the best of me. The exaggerated importance levels that I had placed on my professional life and career had gotten out of hand, and the Universe had come to collect, to balance out my ledger.

This happened before I understood the ten codes this book is about.

And yet intuitively, before I had created these ten tenants, I knew I was getting high off my own self-importance. I knew that if I didn't immediately put together a plan to start taking care of my mental health and look for the positive in everything, I would continue to decline in that state. And because I corrected my energy so completely, I ended up meeting the right person who would eventually introduce me to my producers for my podcast—which at the time was part of a large podcast network.

Had I started to blame or feel sorry for myself, I would have turned this experience into a nightmare. Because I moved into a positive lifetrack and into gratitude, the experience brought me closer to my friends, family, and life path.

If you continue moving through life without taking radical action toward your higher good, you will lose precious time, and, in some cases, years of your life in lower life paths and frequency states. The stakes are high.

This life is not about perfection—it is about growth, expansion, and the willingness to evolve. So many people fear taking action, locked in rigid, linear ways of living. But what if we were courageous enough to step outside the script that someone else wrote for us?

I believe the difference between living a bland life versus living a passion-filled life has to do with our willingness and openness to change.

Most people change very slowly, but incremental slow change is no longer enough. We are living in a time of accelerated shifts, environmental depletion, and deep polarization. The world no longer has the luxury of slow, passive transformation. We must wake up—radically, urgently, and collectively.

This requires operating from neutral awareness rather than reactive emotion. And most importantly, it requires us to choose love over fear, expansion over contraction, and consciousness over unconsciousness.

If you are reading this, my hope is that you realize the power that you hold. You are a creator, an initiator, and a steward of a new paradigm.

Don't let your ego get the best of you.

CHAPTER 12

Leave Behind a Legacy That You Are Proud Of

What you leave behind is not what is engraved in stone monuments, but what is woven into the lives of others.
—Pericles

What impact do you want to leave behind? What legacy will you create?

Think beyond yourself. What message, contribution, or transformation will you offer to the world? For you are here to contribute to something greater than yourself.

How will you answer that call?

Your life is more than just your individual journey—it's an opportunity to steward something meaningful for others.

In *The Matrix*, the moment Neo takes flight for the first time in the final scene is symbolic—it marks his full embodiment of a higher purpose. He is no longer just an individual; he is a force for change.

Now that you have (hopefully) practiced these ten codes, you will likely have an upper hand compared to those who are still asleep. My intention is for everyone reading this book to direct their energy toward creating a better world, not just focusing entirely on their own personal and often materialistic needs. The real invitation here is to shift from individual success to collective elevation; from *me consciousness* to *we consciousness*.

Yes, it's fun to create a life of comfort and creativity, and yet, for those who have been doing personal development work for a while, we all know that financial and material wealth is not a long-term fix. This lesson has been a theme throughout the book for good reason.

Since the dominant purpose to keep people in the matrix—as in the unconscious system that keeps us in a perpetual dream-like state of blindingly living our lives according to how society deems fit—is largely about wealth and control, this is one of the hardest illusions to walk away from. But this is the distinction between those who lead their lives with deep wells of intimacy, curiosity, and connection and those who live their lives based on fear.

Every time I go back to NYC, a place where I lived for over ten years of my life, I'm astounded by how many people believe that success is defined as personal material wealth. Speaking solely about food, clothing, and real estate purchases reflects the pursuit of many people living in this construct of reality.

True success is about waking up elated in the morning and doing what you love to do—without anyone telling you to do it—and thinking about how you can be of service to the whole. Thinking only about serving one's own life is a road to loneliness and depression.

The real freedom in this life is about having agency over one's life outside of the matrix. It's about being pulled by a vision greater than yourself, rather than reacting to day-to-day concerns. Freedom isn't just financial—it's the ability to choose how to spend your time, where to focus energy, and what to create.

The world is shifting, and the future belongs to those who recognize that true prosperity comes not from hoarding resources or winning at the expense of others but from cocreating, from stewarding the planet, and from thinking in terms of win-win realities rather than zero-sum illusions. Every choice we make, every innovation, every creation should not only serve our individual well-being but also contribute to the whole.

Imagine a world where businesses, relationships, and entire economies operate on this principle—where success is measured not by how much we take but by how much we uplift. Where the Earth itself is not seen as a resource to be exploited but as a living, breathing entity we are entrusted to protect. As George Bernard Shaw so powerfully reminds us, "this is the true joy in life, the being used for a purpose recognized by yourself as a mighty one…the being a force of Nature instead of a feverish selfish little clod of ailments and grievances complaining that the world will not devote itself to making you happy." We are capable of so much in this life; it'd be a waste not to leave your mark.

The path forward is about the whole. How can you step into the role of a conscious creator, a steward of life, a force for transformation? Instead of reacting to the world's chaos and script, *be* the presence and the steward that those around you need. Instead of seeking control, align with the rhythm of something far greater than yourself.

Ask yourself, *How does my vision and what I create serve the whole?* And to take it a step further, how can you align your life with the cycles and seasons of the earth and nature?

Throughout history, numerous ancient civilizations have recognized the profound connection between humanity and the cosmos, and aligned their societies with universal laws and natural harmony. The ancient Egyptians, for instance, centered their worldview on Maat, a concept embodying truth, harmony, order, and justice. Maat was also a goddess, representing the cosmic order that the Egyptians sought to maintain through their actions and societal structures.

In the Indian tradition, the notion of *dharma* encompasses duties and ethics aligned with the cosmic order, guiding individuals to live in harmony with the Universe. This principle underscores the importance of righteous living and the interconnectedness of all beings.

Ancient beliefs like these underscore a universal understanding: True fulfillment arises not from isolated, individual pursuits but from aligning oneself with the broader, harmonious rhythms of the Universe. By embracing a cosmic-centric mindset, we become guardians of the Earth, fostering a collective consciousness that transcends personal gain and seeks the well-being of all.

Expand with the Universe

In 1929, Edwin Hubble discovered that the Universe is not static—it is expanding. Galaxies are moving outward, space itself is stretching, and everything in existence is in a state of constant growth and evolution. Expansion is the fundamental nature of the cosmos.

And yet, while the Universe expands, most humans choose contraction. They contract by clinging to materialism, engaging in wars, polluting the oceans, and destroying nature. They resist the very flow of the Universe, moving against the natural order instead of expanding with it. They choose fear over possibility, scarcity over abundance, and isolation over connection.

But the invitation remains. The call to expand is ever present.

To expand with the Universe means to embrace growth, possibility, and higher consciousness. It means shifting from self-interest to collective stewardship, from extraction to regeneration, from division to unity. It means living in harmony with nature and understanding that true wealth is measured not by what we accumulate but by what we contribute.

So, as the Universe expands, will you expand with it? Will you align yourself with the infinite flow of creation, stepping into your highest potential and cocreating a future of harmony, wisdom, and light with your fellow enlightened truth-seekers? This perspective encourages us to view success as a shared journey, where every action contributes to the collective harmony, much like the ancient civilizations that thrived by living in accordance with universal laws.

This is the moment to move beyond the small self into the vast, interconnected reality that has always been calling you. The world doesn't need more people chasing success—it needs more people illuminating the way forward for others and inspiring others to create a vision that excites them every day.

Because I don't know about you, but I want to pass my own torch on in the hope that it will burn brighter than when I first received it.

What Happens When You Follow These Ten Codes?
My hope is that by now, like Neo, you've recognized the larger illusion for what it is. You've stared eye to eye with the matrix.

If you follow these rules and apply them, the world you once struggled against, the obstacles that once seemed insurmountable, the limitations that felt unbreakable—they all start to look different.

Because now you see through the false reality.

When you follow these ten codes, you stop reacting and start creating. You begin to notice that *your energy*—not effort, not struggle, not external validation—is what determines the reality you experience.

Your relationships transform. Instead of chasing, convincing, or proving, you attract. You become magnetic—to love, to opportunities, to the right people. You move through life with clarity and ease because you are no longer operating from scarcity or fear. You become the main character of your life, rather than playing a supporting role in someone else's.

Your purpose becomes clear. Whether it's being a devoted husband and father, managing a non-profit, leading a movement, or creating something entirely new, you are no longer *searching*for meaning—you are *living* it. You are embodying your mission in real time.

You stop trying to force life and start flowing with it. The hustle mentality, the idea that you have to "grind" your way to success, fades away. Instead, you operate from energetic alignment. You move with the current rather than against it.

Your self-concept evolves. You stop seeing yourself as someone who "wants" and start seeing yourself as someone who is. Certainty replaces doubt. You realize that reality is a mirror, reflecting not what you hope for but what you embody.

You no longer fear setbacks. Calamity strikes, life throws its curveballs, but now you know how to navigate it differently. You don't spiral, because you understand that every challenge is an invitation to expand your energy, shift your perception, and step into a higher level of mastery.

Your energy starts flowing. When you drop importance, you stop repelling what you want. The second you stop grasping, doubting, or fearing, your energy stabilizes. And when your energy stabilizes, reality flows effortlessly in your favor.

Harmony between the heart and the mind is the sweet spot where you no longer think of your desires as something "out there" to chase but as something already aligned with who you are. When your mind's focus (thoughts) and your heart's knowing (feeling state) match, the external world has no choice but to rearrange itself around you.

The system wants you obsessed, desperate, and emotionally hooked—because the moment you think you *need* something, you become controlled by it. That's how the matrix works. It feeds off of attachment, keeping you locked in cycles of craving, over-exerting yourself, and a fear of loss.

Here's a new ritual and prompt you can ask yourself each morning, before you reach for your phone, and throughout the day: Ask yourself, *Am I directing my day, or am I drifting into someone else's storyline?*

And now, you can see through the matrix and into the real word—the one that you create.

Bonus Code: Becoming Awareness

Once you've mastered the codes, you can objectively watch yourself from a distance. Think of yourself as a camera lens with no opinion about which scenes are playing out. You can decide what you give meaning to, but you can also zoom out and watch the whole thing for what it is.

Zoom out, and pretend you're watching yourself from the ceiling or further out, from an airplane or even in outer space. In this space, you are not you. You are *awareness*, watching yourself.

But this mastery requires a deep commitment to the path of nonattachment and is not something that is easily mastered. It is an experience that goes beyond one's energy mastery, into a space of the non-linear—the otherworldly. A space where, as Dr. Ibrahim Karim and his daughter Doreya unpacked on my show, there is no such thing as an "afterlife" but rather an "other-life," a continuous field of consciousness that exists beyond the limits of time and form.

In his work, Dr. Ibrahim describes this "other-life" not as a distant realm but as a subtle dimension that coexists with our own, accessible through resonance, harmony, and alignment with divine geometric principles.

Others call this space "zero-point," a place beyond duality.

Once you're in this space, you are untouchable, because you're in a state of neutrality and oneness with all creation. This neutrality is reflective of true energy mastery.

Conclusion

Why do you stay in prison when the door is so wide open?

—Rumi

Having sovereignty over our own energy is our birthright. No one—no system, no person, no external force—has the right to control, extract, or manipulate our energy for their own gain. We are not here to be in unconscious service to others at the expense of ourselves.

Our energy is sacred currency, and how we direct it should be a deliberate, intentional act, rooted in alignment, choice, and self-honor. Of course, we can share our energy generously when it feels aligned and in service to our highest good, but we should never share it as a result of manipulation, guilt, or obligation.

True empowerment comes from recognizing that our energy is ours to cultivate, protect, and expand—and that when we stand in our own energetic autonomy, we become the most powerful versions of ourselves.

You Are The One

The moment Neo realized he was The One, he changed. The matrix didn't suddenly stop being a system designed to control. The agents didn't disappear. The rules of the game were still in place—he just stopped playing by them.

And that's where you are now.

You've spent this journey learning how to master your energy, shift your frequency, and break free from the unconscious programming that's been running your life.

You've seen how reality isn't something that just happens to you—it's something you shape. Not by force, not by grinding harder or changing your external reality, but by becoming a conscious creator, a "main character," of your own field of energy. By noticing what thoughts and feelings you're sharing with the great world mirror.

You don't attract what you want. You attract what you *are*. And now, you know how to align who you are with what you desire.

The world around you won't hand you freedom—it will keep throwing distractions, doubts, and illusions your way. But now you see the illusion. Now you know you have a choice.

You are The One in your life. And no one is coming to wake you up. No one is handing you the red pill. You have to choose it, over and over again.

So, the question is: *Will you choose it—again and again?*

Because the matrix is still running. The simulation is still in place. The system still wants you asleep.

But now—you see through it. You see the glitch. You can treat the illusion with seriousness, or you can treat it with lightness, levity, and humor.

Because once you've seen the simulation for what it is, you can decide right here, right now, to never go back.

And you can promise yourself that you will honor your life path, on your terms, always.

You can promise yourself that moving forward, you will not betray yourself.

You are The One.

You are The One you've been waiting for.

Resources

3HO International. "Sadhana: Daily Spiritual Practice." 3HO
International. Accessed October 1, 2025.
https:// www.3ho.org/ article/ sadhana-daily-spiritual-practice/

Allyn, Rachel. "The Important Difference Between Emotions
and Feelings." *Psychology* Today, February 23, 2022.
https:// www.psychologytoday.com/ us/blog/ the-pleasure-is-all-
yours/ 202202/the-important-difference-between-emotions-and-
feelings

American Psychological Association (APA). "Clinical Practice
Guideline for the Treatment of Posttraumatic Stress Disorder
(PTSD) in Adults." American Psychological Association, 2017.
https:// www.apa.org/ptsd-guideline

Andersone, Nelda. "Understanding the Inner Critic."
Psychology Today. December 15, 2023.
https:// www.psychologytoday.com/ us/blog/ human-inner-
dynamics/202312/understanding-the-inner-critic

Bell, J. S. "On the Einstein-Podolsky-Rosen Paradox." *Physics
PhysiqueFizika* 1, no. 3 (1964): 195–200.
https:// doi.org/10.1103/ PhysicsPhysiqueFizika.1.195

Bentley, Tanya G. K., Gina D'Andrea-Penna, Marina Rakic, Nick Arce, Michelle LaFaille Rachel Berman, et al. "Breathing Practices for Stress and Anxiety Reduction: Conceptual Framework of Implementation Guidelines Based on a Systematic Review of the Published Literature." *Brain Science* 13, no. 12 (2023): 1612. https:/ / doi.org/10.3390/ brainsci13121612

Blavatsky, Helena P. *The Secret Doctrine: The Synthesis of Science, Religion, and Philosophy.* Aryan Theosophical Press, 1888. https:// www.google.com/books/ edition/ The_Secret_Doctrine/7 kNPAQAAIAAJ?hl=en&gbpv=0

Bohm, David. *Wholeness and the Implicate Order.* Routledge & Kegan Paul, 1980.

Cameron, Julia. *The Artist's Way: A Spiritual Path to Higher Creativity (Anniversary ed.).* TarcherPerigee, 2016: 26.

Castaneda, Carlos. *The Fire from Within.* Simon & Schuster, 1984.

Chamberlin, Kent, Wayne Smith, Christopher Chirgqin, Seshank Appasani, and Paul Rioux. "Analysis of the Charge Exchange Between the Human Body and Ground: Evaluation of 'Earthing' From an Electrical Perspective." *Journal of Chiropractic Medicine* 13, no. 4 (December 2014): 239–246. https:// doi.org/10.1016/ j.jcm.2014.10.001

Cherry, Kendra. "What Is Self-Concept?" Very Well Mind, updated on July 29, 2024. https:// www.verywellmind.com/what-is-self-concept-2795865

Christakis, Nicholas A., and James H. Fowler. "The Collective Dynamics of Smoking in a Large Social Network." *The New England Journal of Medicine* 358, no. 21 (2008): 2249–2258. https:// doi.org/10.1056/ NEJMsa0706154

Christakis, Nicholas. A., James H. Fowler. *Connected: The Surprising Power of Our Social Networks and How They Shape Our Lives.* Little, Brown, 2009.

Christakis, Nicholas A., and James H. Fowler. "The Spread of Obesity in a Large Social Network Over 32 Years." *The New England Journal of Medicine* 357, no. 4 (2007): 370–379. https:// doi.org/10.1056/ NEJMsa066082

Community for Conscious Living. "BioGeometry—Measuring the Life Force of the Earth with Dr. Ibrahim Karim." Community for Conscious Living. Dec 27, 2023. https:// communityforconsciousliving.com/ biogeometry-measuring-the-life-force-of-the-earth-with-dr-ibrahim-karim-2/

Datta, Karuna, Anna Bhutambare, Mamatha V. L., Yogita Narawa, Rajagopal Srinath, and Madhuri Kanitkar. "Improved Sleep, Cognitive Processing and Enhanced Learning and Memory Task Accuracy with Yoga Nidra Practice in Novices." *PLOS ONE* 18, no. 12 (2023): e0294678. https:// doi.org/10.1371/ journal.pone.0294678

Derschowitz, Jessica. "Heath Ledger's 'Joker' Diary Revealed in New Documentary." *Entertainment Weekly. Time.* August 10, 2025. https://time.com/ 3990450/heath-ledger-joker-diary/

Disney, Walt, prod., and David Hand, dir. *Snow White and the Seven Dwarfs.* Walt Disney Productions, 1937.

Editors of *Encyclopaedia Britannica*, The. "Cross." *Encyclopaedia Brittanica.* Accessed October 6, 2025. https:// www.britannica.com/ topic/cross-religious-symbol

Editors of *Encyclopaedia Britannica*, The. "Dharma—Religious Concept." *Encyclopaedia Britannica.* Accessed October 20, 2025. https:// www.britannica.com/ topic/ dharma-religious-concept

Editors of *Encyclopaedia Britannica*, The. "Maat—Egyptian Religious Concept." *Encyclopaedia Britannica.* Accessed October 7, 2025. https:// www.britannica.com/topic/ maat-Egyptian-religious-concept

Etienne, Vanessa. "Adrien Brody Developed an Eating Disorder, PTSD After Weight Loss for *The Pianisti: 'Necessary for Storytelling'*." *People.* December 24, 2024. https:// people.com/ adrien-brody-developed-an-eating-disorder-after-the-pianist-weight-loss-8766378

Fasullo, Lisa, Alina Hernandez, & Bodeker, Gerard. "The Innate Human Potential of Elevated and Ecstatic States of Consciousness: Examining Freeform Dance as a Means of Access." *Dance, Movement & Spiritualities* 6, no. 1–2 (Jul 2020): 89–117. https:// doi.org/10.1386/ dmas_00005_1

Ferguson, R. James. "The Ancient Egyptian Concept of Maat: Reflections on Social Justice and Natural Order." Research paper series: Centre for East-West Cultural & Economic Studies, no. 15. Bond University.

https:// research.bond.edu.au/en/publications/the-ancient-egyptian-concept-of-maat-reflections-on-social-justic

Freud, Sigmund. *The Standard Edition of the Complete Psychological Works of Sigmund Freud, Volume IV (1900): The Interpretation of Dreams (First Part)*. Translated by James Strachey. Hogarth Press, 2012.

Garcia, Renée. *Quantum Capitalist: A Revolution of Self, Wealth, and Reality.* Independently published, 2024.

Ghiyam, David. *The David Ghiyam Podcast.* Podcast. "Ep. 9 Certainty: The Key to Manifesting Miracles and Success." November 19, 2024. https:// open.spotify.com/episode/ 1xxyzkZiQXlBlp5KN69zdD?si=9Dp0OiSZStKhMpBEH4f3nQ

Goddard, Neville. *Feeling Is the Secret.* BN Publishing, 1944.

Goddard, Neville. "Gifts Bestowed by God." Lecture, June 4, 1971. Transcript. Internet Archive. https:// archive.org/stream/ NevilleGoddard001/ gifts_bestowed_by_god_djvu.txt

Goddard, Neville. *The Law and the Promise.* DeVorss Publications, 1984.

Goddard, Neville. "Neville Goddard Lectures: 'Eternal States.'" Lecture, September 9, 1968. Transcript. Cool Wisdom Books. https:// / coolwisdombooks.com/ neville/eternal-states/

Goddard, Neville. "Order Your Conversations Aright." Lecture. Transcript. Accessed October 6, 2025. CoolWisdomBooks.

https:// coolwisdombooks.com/neville/neville-goddard-lectures-order-your-conversations-aright/

Goddard, Neville. (1968). "Partakers of the Divine Nature." Lecture, December 6, 1968. Transcript. CoolWisdomBooks. https:// coolwisdombooks.com/neville/neville-goddard-partakers-of-the-divine-nature-1968/

Goddard, Neville. *The Power of Awareness.* Devorss & Company, 1952. https:/ / coolwisdombooks.com/neville/neville-goddard-the-power-of-awareness-1952-full-book/

Gordon-Levitt, Joseph. "How Craving Attention Makes You Less Creative." TED Talk, April 2019. 13 min., 5 sec. https:// www.ted.com/talks/ joseph_gordon_levitt_how_craving_attention_makes_you_less_creative

Harris, Destiny S. "Your Income Is the Average of the 5 People Closest to You." *Medium.* October 5, 2022. https:// medium.datadriveninvestor.com/your-income-is-the-average-of-the-5-people-closest-to-you-4d6c3b70f3ed

Hatfield, Elaine, John T. Cacioppo, and Richard L. Rapson. *Emotional Contagion: Studies in Emotion and Social Interaction.* Cambridge University Press, 1994.

HeartMath Institute. "Heart Coherence." HeartMath Institute. Accessed October 6, 2025. https:// www.heartmath.org/ heart-coherence/

HeartMath Institute. "The Science of HeartMath." HeartMath Institute. Accessed October 6, 2025. https:// www.heartmath.com/ science/#

Hemi-Sync. "Home." Interstate Industries, Inc. (d/ b/ a Hemi-Sync®). Accessed October 1, 2025. https:// hemi-sync.com/

Hillier, Susan, and Anthea Worley. "The Effectiveness of the Feldenkrais Method: A Systematic Review of the Evidence." *Evidence-Based Complementary and Alternative Medicine* (April 8, 2015): 752160. https:// doi.org/ 10.1155/ 2015/752160

Idel, Moshe. *Kabbalah: New Perspectives.* Yale University Press, 1988.

Johnson, Scott A. "How to Incorporate Essential Oils into Your Spiritual Practice." MindBodyGreen, April 30, 2021. https:// www.mindbodygreen.com/ articles/ the-science-of-essential-oils-for-mind-body-and-spirit

Judith, Anodea. *Wheels of Life: A User's Guide to the Chakra System.* Llewellyn Publications, 1999.

Jung, Carl G. *The Collected Works of C. G. Jung, Vol. 9, Part 1: The Archetypes and the Collective Unconscious.* Edited and translated by Gerhard Adler and R. F. C. Hull. Princeton University Press, 1980.

Kabbalah Centre. "Having Certainty." OneHouse. Kabbalah. May 5, 2015. https:// onehouse.kabbalah.com/en/articles/having-certainty

Karim, Ibrahim. "Introduction to Biogeometry." Biogeometry. Accessed October 1, 2025. https:// www.biogeometry.ca/ introduction-to-biogeometry

.

Kerschberg, Zachary, dir. *A Star in the Desert.* Written by Yasmeen Turayhi. A Star in the Desert, LLC, 2020. https:// www.astarinthedesert.com/film

Krishnamurti. "The Source of Conflict." (Public talk.) April 3, 1977, Ojai, CA. Krishnamurti: The Portal. Transcript and video, 1:2:55. https:// www.krishnamurti.org/ transcript/the-source-of-conflict/

Kross, Ethan. *Chatter: The Voice in Our Head, Why It Matters, and How to Harness It.* Crown, 2021.

Kuhfuß, Marie, Tobias Maldei, Andreas Hetmanek, and Nicola Baumann. "Somatic Experiencing—Effectiveness and Key Factors of a Body-Oriented Trauma Therapy: A Scoping Literature Review." *European Journal of Psychotraumatology* 12, no. 1 (July 12, 2021): 1929023. https:// doi.org/10.1080/ 20008198.2021.1929023

Kundalini Research Institute. "About Kundalini Yoga." Kundalini Research Institute. Accessed October 12, 2025. https:// kundaliniresearchinstitute.org/en/ about-kundalini-yoga/

Madame Gandhi. "Why We Must Stop Dancing to the Sound of Our Own Oppression." TED Talk, July 2020. 5 min., 54 sec. https:// www.ted.com/talks/ madame_gandhi_why_we_must_stop_dancing_to_the_sound_of_our_own_oppression

Maisel, Eric. *Coaching the Artist Within: Advice for Writers, Actors, Visual Artists, and Musicians from America's Foremost Creativity Coach.* New World Library, 2005.

Mandelbrot, Benoit B. *The Fractal Geometry of Nature.* W. H. Freeman, 1982.

McCartney, Francesca. "An Empirical Study of the Transmission of Healing Energy via the Internet." *Subtle Energies and Energy Medicine* 18, no. 2 (2017): 21–33. https:// journals.sfu.ca/seemj/ index.php/seemj/ article/ view/ 398

McCartney, Francesca. *Intuition Medicine: The Science of Energy.* Intuition Library Publishing, 2001.

McCraty, Rollin. "Following the Rhythm of the Heart: Heartmath Institute's Path To HRV Biofeedback." *Applied Psychophysiology and Biofeedback* 47, no. 4 (2022): 305–316. https:// doi.org/10.1007/ s10484-022-09554-2

McDermott, R., James H. Fowler, and Nicholas A. Christakis. "Breaking Up Is Hard to Do, Unless Everyone Else Is Doing It Too: Social Network Effects on Divorce in a Longitudinal Sample." *Social Forces,* 92, no. 2 (2013): 491–519. https:// doi.org/10.1093/ sf/ sot096

Melchizedek, Drunvalo. *The Ancient Secret of the Flower of Life, Vol. 1.* Light Technology Publishing, 1999.

Melchizedek, Drunvalo. *The Ancient Secret of the Flower of Life, Vol. 2.* Light Technology Publishing, 2000.

Melchizedek, Drunvalo. *Living in the Heart: How to Enter into the Sacred Space within the Heart.* Light Technology Publishing, 2003.

Moyer, Christopher A., James Rounds, and James W. Hannum. "A Meta-Analysis of Massage Therapy Research."

Psychological Bulletin 130 no. 1 (2004): 3–18. https:// doi.org/10.1037/ 0033-2909.130.1.3

National Qigong Association. "What Is Qigong?" National Qigong Association. Accessed October 1, 2025. https:// www.nqa.org/ what-is-qigong

Olivelle, Patrick, trans. & ed. *The Early Upaniṣads.* Oxford University Press, 1998.

Oschman, J. L., G. Chevalier, and R. Brown. "The Effects of Grounding (Earthing) on Inflammation, the Immune Response, Wound Healing, and Prevention and Treatment of Chronic Inflammatory and Autoimmune Diseases." *Journal of Inflammation Research* 8 (2015): 83–96. https:/ / doi.org/ 10.2147/ JIR.S69656

Pearsall, Paul. *The Heart's Code: Tapping the Wisdom and Power of Our Heart Energy.* Broadway Books, 1998.

Pearsall, P., G. E. Shwartz, and L. G. Russek. "Changes in Heart Transplant Recipients that Parallel the Personalities of Their Donors." *Integrative Medicine* 2, no. 2 (March 21, 2000): 65–72. https:// doi.org/10.1016/ s1096-2190(00)00013-5

Plano, Catherine. "You Are the Average of the Five People You Spend Time With." Ellevate. Accessed October 1, 2025. https:// www.ellevatenetwork.com/ articles/9895-you-are-the-average-of-the-five-people-you-spend-time-with

Psychology Today. "Identity." *Psychology Today.* Accessed August 29, 2025. https:// www.psychologytoday.com/ us/basics/ identity

Rumi, Jalāl al-Dīn. *The Essential Rumi.* Translated by Coleman Barks. New York: HarperOne, 1995.

Shapiro, Francine. *Eye Movement Desensitization and Reprocessing (EMDR): Basic Principles, Protocols, and Procedures.* Guilford Press, 2002.

Shaw, George Bernard. *Man and Superman: A Comedy and a Philosophy.* 1903. Project Gutenberg. Updated July 30, 2015. https:// www.gutenberg.org/ files/3328/3328-h/ 3328-h.htm

Scholem, Gershom. *Major Trends in Jewish Mysticism.* Schocken Books, 1995.

Simon, Naomi M., Stefan G. Hofmann, David Rosenfield, Susanne S. Hoeppner, Elizabeth A. Hoge, Eric Bui, et al. "Efficacy of Yoga vs Cognitive Behavioral Therapy and Stress Education for Generalized Anxiety Disorder: A Randomized Clinical Trial." *JAMA Psychiatry* 78, no. 1 (2021): 13–20. https:// doi.org/10.1001/ jamapsychiatry.2020.2496

Sinatra, Stephen T., Sharon Whiteley, and Step Sinatra. *Get Grounded, Get Well: Connect to the Earth to Improve Your Health, Well-Being, and Energy.* Red Wheel/ Weiser, 2023.

Sissons, Beth. "What Is Birth Order Theory?" *Medical News Today.* May 14, 2024. https:// www.medicalnewstoday.com/ articles/ birth-order-theory

Spira, Rupert. "Time Is Never Actually Experienced." Lecture. Buckland Hall, Wales, spring 2017. Posted Dec 14, 2018, by Rupert Spira, YouTube. Video, 12 min., 55 sec. https:// www.youtube.com/ watch?v=LjDhov4p6Sg

St. Germain, Maureen. Workshop presented at the Conscious Life Expo, Los Angeles, CA, 2022.

Stanislavski, Constantin. *An Actor Prepares.* Albatross Publishers, 2022.

Strogatz, Steven. *Sync: How Order Emerges from Chaos in the Universe, Nature and Daily Life.* Grand Central Publishing, 2004.

Thébault, Bertrand. "Reality Occurs Only in the Eternal Now: Time Collapses to the casual origin Treal=0." July 2025. https:// www.researchgate.net/publication/ 393442493_Reality_occurs_only_in_the_eternal_now_Time_collapses_to_the_causal_origin_Treal0

TRE for All. "What Is TRE®?" TRE for All. Accessed August 1, 2025. https:// treglobal.org/what-is-tre/

Turayhi, Yasmeen, host. *Gateways to Awakening.* Podcast. "The 12 Keys to Creativity and How to Live a Creative Life with Eric Maisel." Produced by Hakawati. May 20, 2021. https:// hakawati.fm/podcast/ episode/413898

Turayhi, Yasmeen, host. *Gateways to Awakening.* Podcast. "Biogeometry & Time: How Shapes, Symbols and Resonance Re-Center Our Homes with Doreya Karim." Produced by Hakawati. October 15, 2025. https:// open.spolify.com/episode/ 2cba6G004rFkD7r986HQvp?si=CUqWkUBaQj2lwSbpfB4mgw

Turayhi, Yasmeen, host. *Gateways to Awakening.* Podcast. "The Chakras, Creativity and the Energy Body and 'She Rises'

with Anodea Judith." Produced by Hakawati. October 5, 2023.
https:// hakawati.fm/podcast/ episode/479607

Turayhi, Yasmeen, host. *Gateways to Awakening*. Podcast.
"Conscious Music Consumption and Why Your Voice Matters
with Madame Gandhi." Produced by Hakawati.
https:// hakawati.fm/podcast/ episode/479783

Turayhi, Yasmeen, host. *Gateways to Awakening*. Podcast.
"Flower of Life and Connecting with the Heart with Viola Rose."
Produced by Hakawati. January 1, 2025.
https:// hakawati.fm/podcast/ episode/490846

Turayhi, Yasmeen, host. *Gateways to Awakening*. Podcast.
"Grounding. What Is It, Benefits, How It Reduces Inflammation
and Helps You Heal, with Step Sinatra." Produced by Hakawati.
October 15, 2020. https://hakawati.fm/ podcast/episode/ 243036

Turayhi, Yasmeen, host. *Gateways to Awakening*. Podcast.
"The Healing Power of Sound and Binaural Beats with Elizabeth
Krasnoff." Produced by Hakawati. November 5, 2020.
https:// hakawati.fm/podcast/ episode/252806

Turayhi, Yasmeen, host. *Gateways to Awakening*. Podcast.
"Heart Coherence with the Heart-Math Institute founding CEO,
Bruce Cryer." Produced by Hakawati. April 23, 2025.
https:// open.spotify.com/episode/ 6nW9QxkG8kqetBCPZ6EQW
7

Turayhi, Yasmeen, host. *Gateways to Awakening*. Podcast.
"How to Be a 'Quantum Capitalist' and Unhook from the Matrix

with Renée Garcia." Produced by Hakawati. August 29, 2024. https:// hakawati.fm/podcast/ episode/487802

Turayhi, Yasmeen, host. *Gateways to Awakening.* Podcast. "How to Connect with the Cosmic Energy Blueprint: Yoga, Star Portals, Meridians, and More with Yogeshwara Pradeep Ullal from Himalayan Kriya Yoga." Produced by Hakawati. May 7, 2025. https:// open.spotify.com/episode/ 6O3rcU2qucyo5YW4SVCw65 ?si=Raes7OdpSLeDJwWAKCF-ww

Turayhi, Yasmeen, host. *Gateways to Awakening.* Podcast. "How to Deal with the Voice in Your Head and Inner Critic with Ethan Kross." Produced by Hakawati. March 17, 2022. https:// hakawati.fm/podcast/ episode/466182

Turayhi, Yasmeen, host. *Gateways to Awakening.* Podcast. "How to Find the Key to Your Body's Natural Repair System with Brandy Gillmore." Produced by Hakawati. July 11, 2024. https:// hakawati.fm/podcast/ episode/486592

Turayhi, Yasmeen, host. *Gateways to Awakening.* Podcast. "How to Shift Your Layer of Reality with Reality Transurfing and Renée Garcia." Produced by Hakawati. September 14, 2023. https:// hakawati.fm/podcast/ episode/479075

Turayhi, Yasmeen, host. *Gateways to Awakening.* Podcast. "How to Understand Your Emotions and What They're Telling You with Karla McLaren." Produced by Hakawati. February 3, 2022. https:// hakawati.fm/ podcast/ episode/461350

Turayhi, Yasmeen, host. *Gateways to Awakening*. Podcast. "The Power of Values, Gratitude, and Destiny with Dr. John DeMartini." Produced by Hakawati. February 26, 2025. https:// open.spotify.com/episode/ 5lZqrfbwUrDqPa8m7RsX57

Turayhi, Yasmeen, host. *Gateways to Awakening*. Podcast. "The Quirks of the Quantum Mind with the Princeton Engineering Lab with Brenda Dunn." December 30, 2021. https:// hakawati.fm/podcast/ episode/ 456460

Turayhi, Yasmeen, host. *Gateways to Awakening*. Podcast. "Scripting Your Future Self with Royce Christyn." Produced by Hakawati. December 22, 2022. https:// hakawati.fm/podcast/ episode/ 472500

Turayhi, Yasmeen, host. *Gateways to Awakening*. Podcast. "Shadow Work and the Inner Work of Age with Connie Zweig Ph.D." Produced by Hakawati. April 21, 2022. https:// hakawati.fm/podcast/ episode/ 467049

Turayhi, Yasmeen, host. *Gateways to Awakening*. Podcast. "Why the Body Needs to Move, a Conversation about Movement with Beth Riley." Produced by Hakawati. September 2, 2021. https:// hakawati.fm/podcast/ episode/ 434562

Turayhi, Yasmeen. *A Star in the Desert: A Short Story*. A Star in the Desert LLC, 2019. https:// www.astarinthedesert.com/book

Tzu, Laozi. 1963. *Tao Te Ching*. Translated by D. C. Lau. Penguin Books, 1963.

Van Bakel, Rogier. "Mind over Matter." WIRED. April 1, 1995. https:// www.wired.com/1995/04/ pear/

Van der Kolk, Bessel. *The Body Keeps the Score: Brain, Mind, and Body in the Healing of Trauma*. Penguin Books, 2015.

Vazza, F., and A. Feletti. "The Quantitative Comparison Between the Neuronal Network and The Cosmic Web." *Frontiers in Physics* 8 (2020): 525731. https:// doi.org/10.3389/ fphy.2020.525731

Veith, Ilza, trans. *Huang Ti Nei Ching Su Wên: The Yellow Emperor's Classic of Internal Medicine*. University of California Press, 1972.

Walker, Heather Celeste. "Ecstatic dance: A depth-psychological exploration of lived experience." PhD diss., Pacifica Graduate Institute, 2020. ProQuest (28544597). https:// www.proquest.com/ openview/ aef3fbd0e90451992c7aafc854083f8e/ 1?cbl=18750&diss=y&pq-origsite=gscholar

Zeland, Vadim. *Reality Transurfing: Steps I–V*. Joanna Dobson, trans. CreateSpace Independent Publishing Platform, 2016.

Acknowledgements

To every mentor, friend, and teacher who has walked this path with me, offering wisdom, encouragement, and belief in what is possible. To the 250-plus podcast guests from Gateways to Awakening who have shared their knowledge and expanded my understanding of intuition, consciousness, and the art of creating reality.

To Dr. Francesca McCartney and the Academy of Intuition Medicine, for guiding me deeper into the unseen realms, and to the great thought leaders, past and present, whose teachings have shaped my journey: Frederick Dodson, Neville Goddard, Rumi, Akasha-Rose Emmanuel, Joseph Murphy, Vadim Zeland, Arielle Ford, Renée Garcia, Tashi Powers, Christine Marie Mason, Jerry Emeka, Jon Amiel, Nikola Tesla, Shakespeare, St. Germain, Alan Watts, and Maya Angelou.

To the gods and goddesses and ancient wisdom keepers who offer us perspective: Saraswati, Lakshmi, Red Tara,

Durga, Kali, Artemis, Aphrodite, Quan Yin, and Thoth, whose divine presences remind me that creation, abundance, and transformation are always within reach. To the Hermetica, the Emerald Tablets, and all the ancient wisdom passed down to us from ancient civilizations that inspired me greatly.

To my time in the ancient temples in Egypt, which inspired me to dig deeper and ask better questions about the nature of reality and the meaning of time.

To the Hakawati team—Karim, Joy and Gina—for believing in me and encouraging me to bring my voice out into the world through my global podcast, Gateways to Awakening.

To those of you who listened to Gateways to Awakening and joined me on this journey of self-inquiry and personal growth, seeking to become better versions of ourselves so we could show up more fully for others, thank you. I'm deeply grateful for you.

To the ones who see through the illusion, the dream-world in which we live in and stay awake. Thank you for joining me on this path in this lifetime and helping others remember.

And to my family, the foundation upon which all things become possible.

This book is for you.

About the Author

Yasmeen Turayhi is the host of the podcast *Gateways to Awakening* and the founder of the Inner Knowing School of Intuition and Energy Mastery. As an award-winning filmmaker, entrepreneur, and longtime product leader, she teaches executives and creatives how to combine intuition, energy mastery, and rigorous craft so they can make better decisions, bolder work, and kinder organizations.

Yasmeen founded the Modern Product Agency and has commercialized more than two hundred technology products across neurotech, climate tech, fintech, and AI. She's the author of three books on product marketing— including her bestseller *Product Marketing Debunked*—and brings a results-driven clarity to spiritual practice: short rituals, somatic resets, and practical frameworks that actually scale.

Her podcast *Gateways to Awakening* explores neuroscience, intuition, and consciousness and ranks in the top 2 percent of podcasts globally on Apple. Yasmeen holds a master certification in intuition medicine and leads trainings through the Inner Knowing School of Intuition that blends research, ritual, and real-world application. Her TEDx talk, "Using Your Intuition to Make Better Decisions," has been viewed more than twenty-five thousand times.

She lives and works between the practical demands of business and the uncanny possibilities of subtle energy, helping readers and listeners reclaim attention, deepen their creative practice, and steward their power with humility.